CB126803

UNLOCK

Second Edition

2

Reading, Writing & Critical Thinking

STUDENT'S BOOK WITH DIGITAL PACK

Richard O'Neill and Michele Lewis
with Chris Sowton, Jennifer Farmer
and Carolyn Flores

CAMBRIDGE
UNIVERSITY PRESS

CAMBRIDGE
UNIVERSITY PRESS

University Printing House, Cambridge CB2 8BS, United Kingdom

One Liberty Plaza, 20th Floor, New York, NY 10006, USA

477 Williamstown Road, Port Melbourne, VIC 3207, Australia

314–321, 3rd Floor, Plot 3, Splendor Forum, Jasola District Centre, New Delhi – 110025, India

103 Penang Road, #05-06/07, Visioncrest Commercial, Singapore 238467

Cambridge University Press is part of the University of Cambridge.

It furthers the University's mission by disseminating knowledge in the pursuit of education, learning and research at the highest international levels of excellence.

www.cambridge.org
Information on this title: www.cambridge.org/9781009031394

First published 2014
Second Edition 2019
Second Edition update published 2021

20 19 18 17 16 15 14 13 12 11

Printed in Malaysia by Vivar Printing

A catalogue record for this publication is available from the British Library

ISBN 978-1-009-03139-4 Reading, Writing and Critical Thinking Student's Book with Digital Pack 2
ISBN 978-1-009-03129-5 Reading, Writing and Critical Thinking Student's eBook with Digital Pack 2

CONTENTS

MAP OF THE BOOK

UNIT	VIDEO	READING	VOCABULARY
1 PLACES Reading 1: Rise of the megacities (Geography) Reading 2: Homestay holidays: a home away from home (Travel and Tourism)	Destination Jakarta	***Key reading skill:*** Scanning for numbers ***Additional skills:*** Understanding key vocabulary Using your knowledge Reading for main ideas Reading for detail Scanning to find information Scanning to predict content Working out meaning from context Making inferences Synthesizing	Vocabulary to describe places (e.g. *cheap, expensive, modern, noisy*)
2 FESTIVALS AND CELEBRATIONS Reading 1: Celebrate! (Sociology) Reading 2: Muscat Festival (Cultural Studies)	New Year celebrations in the UK	***Key reading skill:*** Previewing a text ***Additional skills:*** Understanding key vocabulary Reading for main ideas Reading for detail Recognizing text type Scanning to predict content Synthesizing	Vocabulary to describe festivals (e.g. *culture, highlight, history, lucky, traditional*)
3 THE INTERNET AND TECHNOLOGY Reading 1: Someone's always watching you online ... (Information Technology) Reading 2: Video games for kids: win or lose? (Information Technology)	Predictive advertising	***Key reading skills:*** Reading for main ideas Making inferences ***Additional skills:*** Understanding key vocabulary Scanning to predict content Reading for main ideas Reading for detail Using your knowledge Recognizing text type Synthesizing	Vocabulary to describe the internet and technology (e.g. *a computer program, a smartphone*) Compound nouns
4 WEATHER AND CLIMATE Reading 1: Extreme weather (Geography) Reading 2: Surviving the sea of sand: how to stay alive in the Sahara Desert (Environmental Science)	Tornadoes	***Key reading skills:*** Reading for detail Using your knowledge to predict content ***Additional skills:*** Understanding key vocabulary Reading for main ideas Recognizing text type Synthesizing	Collocations with *temperature* Vocabulary to describe a graph

	GRAMMAR	CRITICAL THINKING	WRITING
	Nouns and adjectives: • Adjectives • Countable and uncountable nouns • Articles: *a*, *an*, zero article Quantifiers ***Grammar for writing:*** Simple sentences 1: Subject + verb *There is / There are*	Evaluating positives and negatives	***Academic writing skills:*** Capital letters and punctuation ***Writing task type:*** Write descriptive sentences ***Writing task:*** Describe the place where you live. Write about its positives and its negatives.
	Prepositions of time and place Adverbs of frequency ***Grammar for writing:*** Simple sentences 2: • Objects and extra information • Prepositional phrases	Identifying important information	***Academic writing skills:*** Organizing sentences into a paragraph ***Writing task type:*** Write a descriptive paragraph ***Writing task:*** Describe a festival or special event.
	Giving opinions ***Grammar for writing:*** Connecting ideas: • *And*, *also* and *too* • Compound sentences • *However*	Identifying appropriate answers	***Academic writing skills:*** Topic sentences ***Writing task type:*** Write a one-sided opinion paragraph ***Writing task:*** The internet wastes our time. It does not help us do more work. Do you agree or disagree?
	Grammar for writing: Comparative and superlative adjectives	Analyzing graphs	***Academic writing skills:*** Topic sentences for descriptive paragraphs about a graph Supporting sentences Giving examples: *like*, *such as* and *for example* ***Writing task type:*** Write a paragraph describing data from graphs ***Writing task:*** Compare the weather in two places, using information from graphs.

UNIT	VIDEO	READING	VOCABULARY	
5 SPORTS AND COMPETITION Reading 1: Five unusual sports (Sports Science) Reading 2: Tough Guy: a race to the limit (Sports Science)	A 96-year-old bungee jumper	***Key reading skill:*** Scanning to predict content ***Additional skills:*** Understanding key vocabulary Previewing Reading for main ideas Reading for detail Recognizing text type Understanding discourse Working out meaning from context Synthesizing	Vocabulary to describe sport	
6 BUSINESS Reading 1: Are you ready for the world of work? (Human Resources) Reading 2: The story of Google (Business)	Amazon's fulfilment centre	***Key reading skills:*** Working out meaning from context Annotating a text ***Additional skills:*** Understanding key vocabulary Skimming Scanning to predict content Reading for main ideas Reading for detail Identifying audience Making inferences Synthesizing	Collocations with *business* Business vocabulary	
7 PEOPLE Reading 1: Incredible people (Sociology) Reading 2: More incredible people (Sociology)	The gold prospector	***Key reading skill:*** Skimming ***Additional skills:*** Understanding key vocabulary Reading for main ideas Reading for detail Working out meaning from context Identifying purpose Making inferences Synthesizing	Adjectives to describe people	
8 THE UNIVERSE Reading 1: The rise of commercial space travel (Space Science) Reading 2: Life on other planets (Space Science)	Going to the International Space Station	***Key reading skill:*** Identifying the author's purpose ***Additional skills:*** Understanding key vocabulary Using your knowledge Reading for main ideas Reading for detail Skimming Making inferences Distinguishing fact from opinion Synthesizing	Vocabulary for giving evidence and supporting an argument	

	GRAMMAR	CRITICAL THINKING	WRITING
	Prepositions of movement *Grammar for writing:* Subject and verb agreement	Analyzing a diagram	*Academic writing skills:* Ordering events in a process Removing unrelated information *Writing task type:* Write a process paragraph *Writing task:* Describe the Sydney Triathlon.
	Grammar for writing: The present simple and the past simple Time clauses with *when* to describe past events	Organizing events in time order	*Academic writing skills:* Adding details to main facts *Writing task type:* Write a narrative paragraph *Writing task:* Write a narrative paragraph about the history of a business.
	Noun phrases with *of* *Grammar for writing:* Modals of necessity	Categorizing ideas	*Academic writing skills:* Concluding sentences *Writing task type:* Write an explanatory paragraph *Writing task:* Who do you think is a good role model? Why? Write a paragraph explaining the qualities that make that person a good role model.
	Grammar for writing: *That* clauses in complex sentences Infinitives of purpose *Because* and *so*	Evaluating arguments	*Academic writing skills:* Essay organization *Writing task type:* Complete an opinion essay *Writing task:* Should governments spend more money on space exploration? Give reasons and examples to support your opinion.

YOUR GUIDE TO UNLOCK

Unlock your academic potential

Unlock Second Edition is a six-level, academic-light English course created to build the skills and language students need for their studies (CEFR Pre-A1 to C1). It develops students' ability to think critically in an academic context right from the start of their language learning. Every level has 100% new inspiring video on a range of academic topics.

Confidence in teaching.

Joy in learning.

Better Learning WITH UNLOCK SECOND EDITION

Better Learning is our simple approach where insights we've gained from research have helped shape content that drives results. We've listened to teachers all around the world and made changes so that *Unlock* Second Edition better supports students along the way to academic success.

CRITICAL THINKING

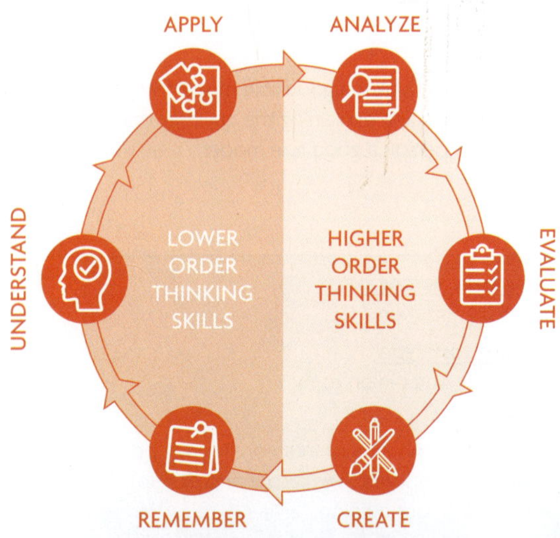

Critical thinking in *Unlock* Second Edition ...

- is **informed** by a range of academic research from Bloom in the 1950s, to Krathwohl and Anderson in the 2000s, to more recent considerations relating to 21st Century Skills
- has a **refined** syllabus with a better mix of higher- and lower-order critical thinking skills
- is **measurable**, with objectives and self-evaluation so students can track their critical thinking progress
- is **transparent** so teachers and students know when and why they're developing critical thinking skills
- is **supported** with professional development material for teachers so teachers can teach with confidence

... so that students have the best possible chance of academic success.

INSIGHT

Most classroom time is currently spent on developing lower-order critical thinking skills. Students need to be able to use higher-order critical thinking skills too.

CONTENT

Unlock Second Edition includes the right mix of lower- and higher-order thinking skills development in every unit, with clear learning objectives.

RESULTS

Students are better prepared for their academic studies and have the confidence to apply the critical thinking skills they have developed.

DIGITAL CLASSROOM MATERIAL

The *Unlock* Second Edition Digital Classroom Material ...

- offers extra, **motivating** practice in speaking, critical thinking and language
- provides a **convenient** bank of language and skills reference informed by our exclusive Corpus research
- is easily **accessible** and **navigable** from students' mobile phones
- is fully **integrated** into every unit
- provides Unlock-**specific** activities to extend the lesson whenever you see this symbol

... so that students can easily get the right, extra practice they need, when they need it.

INSIGHT

The digital classroom material is most effective when it's an integral, well-timed part of a lesson.

CONTENT

Every unit of *Unlock* Second Edition is enhanced with bespoke digital classroom material to extend the skills and language students are learning in the book. The symbol shows when to use the material.

RESULTS

Students are motivated by having relevant extension material on their mobile phones to maximize their language learning. Teachers are reassured that the material adds real language-learning value to their lessons.

RESEARCH

We have gained deeper insights to inform *Unlock* Second Edition by ...

- carrying out **extensive market research** with teachers and students to fully understand their needs throughout the course's development
- consulting **academic research** into critical thinking
- refining our vocabulary syllabus using our **exclusive Corpus research**

... so that you can be assured of the quality of *Unlock* Second Edition.

INSIGHT

- Consultation with global Advisory Panel
- Comprehensive reviews of material
- Face-to-face interviews and Skype™ calls
- Classroom observations

CONTENT

- Improved critical thinking
- 100% new video and video lessons
- Clearer contexts for language presentation and practice
- Text-by-text glossaries
- More supportive writing sections
- Digital workbook with more robust content
- Comprehensive teacher support

RESULTS

"Thank you for all the effort you've put into developing Unlock Second Edition. As far as I can see, I think the new edition is more academic and more appealing to young adults."

Burçin Gönülsen,
Işık Üniversity, Turkey

HOW *UNLOCK* WORKS

Unlock your knowledge

Encourages discussion around the themes of the unit with inspiration from interesting questions and striking images.

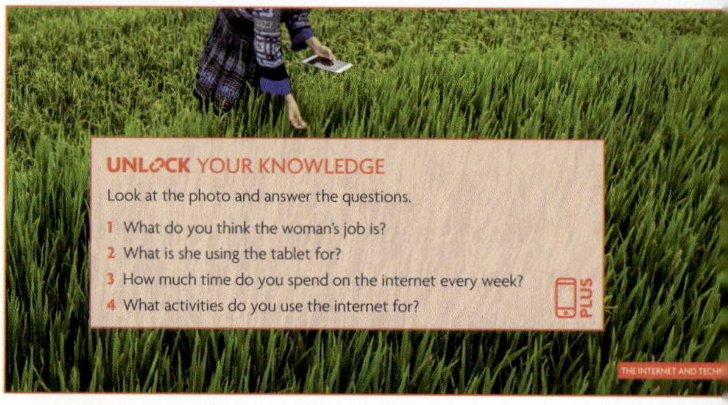

Watch and listen

Features an engaging and motivating video which generates interest in the topic and develops listening skills.

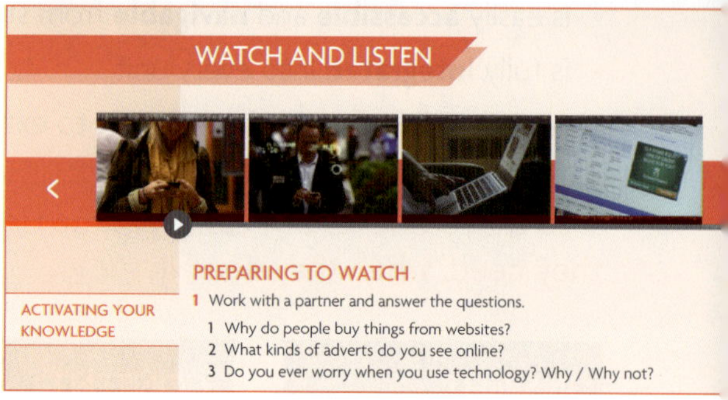

READING

Reading 1

The first text offers students the opportunity to develop the reading skills required to process academic texts, and presents and practises the vocabulary needed to comprehend the text itself.

Reading 2

Presents a second text which provides a different angle on the topic and serves as a model text for the writing task.

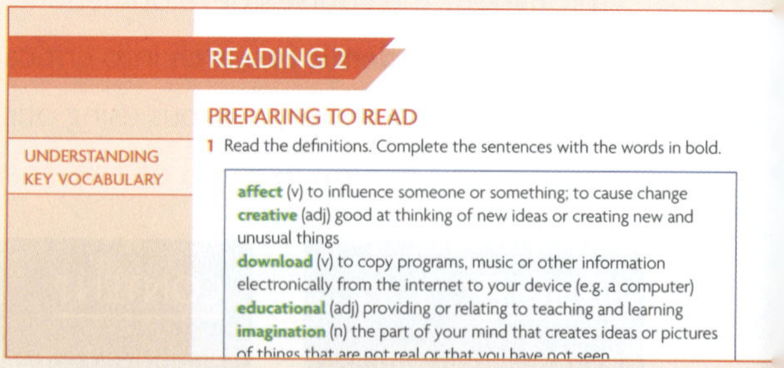

Language development

Consolidates and expands on the language presented in preparation for the writing task.

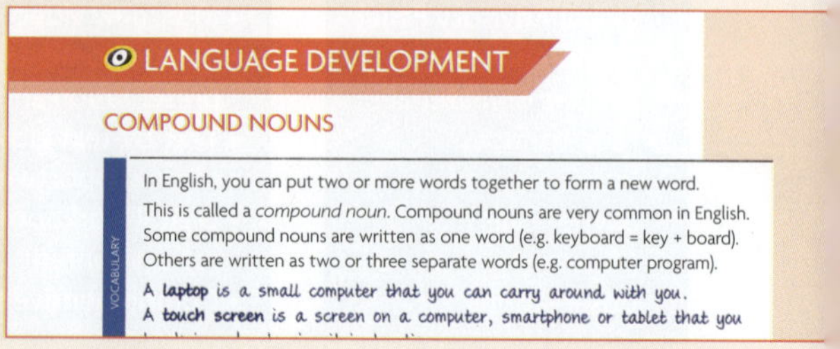

WRITING

Critical thinking

Develops the lower- and higher-order thinking skills required for the writing task.

WRITING

CRITICAL THINKING

At the end of this unit, you will write a one-sided opinion paragraph. Look at this unit's writing task below.

The internet wastes our time. It does not help us do more work. Do you agree or disagree?

Grammar for writing

Presents and practises grammatical structures and features needed for the writing task.

GRAMMAR FOR WRITING

CONNECTING IDEAS

and, *also* and *too*

Use the conjunction *and* or the adverbs *also* or *too* to add information. Connecting ideas makes your writing better and easier to understand.

Use *and* to join two ideas in a single sentence.

My sister has a computer. She has a smartphone.
→ My sister has a computer **and** a smartphone.

Jessica texts her friends. She shares photos.
→ Jessica texts her friends **and** shares photos.

Academic writing skills

Practises all the writing skills needed for the writing task.

ACADEMIC WRITING SKILLS

TOPIC SENTENCES

A topic sentence tells you the main idea of a paragraph. It is usually the first or second sentence in a paragraph. A topic sentence has two parts: the *topic* and the *controlling idea*. The topic tells you what the paragraph is about. The controlling idea gives the topic a focus.

topic *controlling idea*

The internet has many advantages. You can find information quickly

Writing task

Uses the skills and language learned throughout the unit to support students in drafting, producing and editing a piece of academic writing. This is the unit's main learning objective.

WRITING TASK

The internet wastes our time. It does not help us do more work. Do you agree or disagree?

PLAN

1 Look at the question above. Do you agree or disagree? Circle the answer that is true for you.

1 2 3 4

1 = strongly disagree
2 = disagree more than agree
3 = agree more than disagree
4 = strongly agree

2 Look at the table in Exercise 4 of the Critical thinking section. Highlight the three ideas that best support your opinion.

3 Look at the paragraph planner.

1 Write your topic sentence in the planner.

Objectives review

Allows students to evaluate how well they have mastered the skills covered in the unit.

OBJECTIVES REVIEW

1 Check your learning objectives for this unit. Write *3*, *2* or *1* for each objective.

3 = very well 2 = well 1 = not so well

I can …

watch and understand a video about advertising. ____

read for main ideas. ____

make inferences. ____

identify appropriate answers. ____

Wordlist

Lists the key vocabulary from the unit. The most frequent words used at this level in an academic context are highlighted. ⊙

2 Use the *Unlock* Digital Workbook for more practice with this unit's learning objectives.

UNLOCK ONLINE

WORDLIST

area (n) ⊙	countryside (n) ⊙	opportunity (n)
beautiful (adj)	expensive (adj) ⊙	polluted (adj)
boring (adj)	expert (n) ⊙	pollution (n) ⊙
capital (n) ⊙	interesting (adj) ⊙	population (n) ⊙
cheap (adj) ⊙	local (adj) ⊙	quiet (adj)
city centre (n)	modern (adj)	traffic (n) ⊙
clean (adj) ⊙	noisy (adj) ⊙	ugly (adj)

⊙ = high-frequency words in the Cambridge Academic Corpus

COMPONENTS

Unlock offers 56 hours per Student's Book, which is extendable to 90 hours with the Digital Pack, and other additional activities in the Teacher's Manual and Development Pack.

Unlock is a paired-skills course with two separate Student's Books per level. For levels 1–5 (CEFR A1 – C1), these are ***Reading, Writing and Critical Thinking*** and ***Listening, Speaking and Critical Thinking***. They share the same unit topics so you have access to a wide range of material at each level. Each Student's Book provides access to the Digital Pack.

Unlock Basic has been developed for pre-A1 learners. ***Unlock Basic Skills*** integrates reading, writing, listening, speaking and critical thinking in one book to provide students with an effective and manageable learning experience. ***Unlock Basic Literacy*** develops and builds confidence in literacy. The *Basic* books also share the same unit topics and so can be used together or separately, and ***Unlock Basic Literacy*** can be used for self-study.

Student components

Resource	Description	Access
Student's Books	• Levels 1–5 come with the Digital Pack (Digital Workbook, Digital Classroom Material, downloadable audio and video) – Levels 1–4 (8 units) – Level 5 (10 units) • *Unlock Basic Skills* comes with downloadable audio and video (11 units) • *Unlock Basic Literacy* comes with downloadable audio (11 units)	• The Digital Pack (Digital Workbook, Digital Classroom Material, downloadable audio and video) is accessed on our **learning platform** via the unique code inside the front cover of the Student's Book • The audio and video are downloadable from the Student's Resources section on the **learning platform**
Digital Workbook	• Levels 1–5 only • Extension activities to further practise the language and skills learned • All-new vocabulary activities in the Digital Workbook practise the target vocabulary in new contexts	• The Digital Workbook is on our **learning platform** and is accessed via the unique code inside the front cover of the Student's Book
Digital Classroom Material	• Levels 1–5 only • Extra practice in speaking, critical thinking and language	• Please go to **cambridgeone.org** to access the digital classroom material. • Students use the same login details as for the **learning platform**, and then they are logged in for a year
Video	• Levels 1–5 and *Unlock Basic Skills* only • All the video from the course	• The video is downloadable from the Student's Resources section on the **learning platform**
Audio	• All the audio from the course	• The audio is downloadable from the Student's Resources section on the **learning platform**

Teacher components

Resource	Description	Access
Teacher's Manual and Development Pack	• One manual covers Levels 1–5 • It contains flexible lesson plans, lesson objectives, additional activities and common learner errors as well as professional development for teachers, *Developing critical thinking skills in your students* • It comes with downloadable audio and video, vocabulary worksheets and peer-to-peer teacher training worksheets	• The audio, video and worksheets are downloadable from the Teacher Resources section on the **learning platform**
Presentation Plus	• Software for interactive whiteboards so you can present the pages of the Student's Books and easily play audio and video, and check answers	• Presentation Plus is available from the Teacher Resources section on our **learning platform**

LEARNING OBJECTIVES	IN THIS UNIT YOU WILL ...
Watch and listen	watch and understand a video about Jakarta.
Reading skill	scan for numbers.
Critical thinking	evaluate positives and negatives.
Grammar	use nouns and adjectives; use countable and uncountable nouns; use quantifiers; write simple sentences; use *there is / there are*.
Academic writing skill	use capital letters and punctuation.
Writing task	write descriptive sentences.

PLACES UNIT 1

UNLOCK YOUR KNOWLEDGE

Look at the photo and answer the questions.

1 Do you know this city? Which country do you think it is in? How do you know?

2 Is the city similar to or different from the place where you live? In what ways?

3 Would you like to live here? Why / Why not?

PLUS

WATCH AND LISTEN

PREPARING TO WATCH

ACTIVATING YOUR KNOWLEDGE

1 Work in a small group. Discuss the questions.

1 What is the capital city of your country? Is it a popular destination for tourists? Why / Why not?
2 Do you know what a megacity is? What do you think the three biggest megacities in the world are?
3 Which big cities in your country have a harbour? Why are harbours important to cities?

PREDICTING CONTENT USING VISUALS

2 Look at the pictures. Circle all the words you think are true. Compare your answers with a partner.

1 I think this is a city in *Europe* / *Asia* / *Africa*.
2 I think the city is a *megacity* / *popular destination* / *capital city*.
3 I think this city has *an old town* / *a harbour* / *famous restaurants*.

GLOSSARY

destination (n) the place where someone or something is going

harbour (n) an area of water by the coast used to keep ships safe

tower (n) a very tall, thin building, or part of a building

monument (n) a special building to make people remember an event in history or a famous person

goods (n) things that people sell

fireworks (n) small objects that explode to make a loud noise and bright colours in the night sky

WHILE WATCHING

UNDERSTANDING MAIN IDEAS

3 ▶ Watch the video. Check your ideas in Exercise 2.

UNDERSTANDING DETAIL

4 ▶ Watch again. Choose the best answer to each question.

1 How many people live in Jakarta?
 a 9 million b 11 million
2 What style of buildings can you see in the old town?
 a Indonesian b European
3 What can you see at Sunda Kelapa harbour?
 a ships from Europe, China and India b Indonesian ships
4 What is under the national monument?
 a a golden flame b the National Museum
5 What is *soto*?
 a meat and vegetable soup b a fried rice dish
6 When is the fireworks display at Lagoon Beach?
 a every evening b on New Year's Eve

MAKING INFERENCES

5 ▶ Watch again. Work with a partner. Discuss the questions.

1 Why does Jakarta have very busy roads?
2 Why did Jakarta grow into a big city?
3 Why are there European-style buildings in Jakarta?
4 How long have people lived in Indonesia?
5 Who is the video for – tourists or business people? Why?

DISCUSSION

6 Work in a small group. Discuss the questions.

1 Compare Jakarta to another city you know well. How is it similar or different?
2 Imagine you are making a video about your capital city for tourists. What information and places would you include?
3 What different information would you include in a video for business people?

7 When you visit a new place, what is most interesting to you? Order the ideas from 1 (most interesting) to 6 (least interesting). Compare your answers with a partner.

_____ food and drink _____ history _____ shopping
_____ meeting people _____ leisure activities _____ nature

READING

READING 1

PREPARING TO READ

UNDERSTANDING KEY VOCABULARY

1 You are going to read an article about cities. Read the sentences (1–8). Write the words in bold next to the definitions (a–h).

1. More than 4 million people live in Riyadh. Riyadh has the largest **population** in Saudi Arabia.
2. The city hired an **expert** to help decide on the best place for the new shopping centre. He knows a lot about planning big cities.
3. People who live in big cities often visit the **countryside** so they can get away from the crowds and breathe some fresh air.
4. Studying in another country gives students the **opportunity** to learn about new cultures and see how other people live.
5. The sky was so grey with air **pollution** from cars and factory smoke that I couldn't see the sunset.
6. Shanghai is thousands of years old, but it is also a very **modern** city. It is filled with tall glass buildings and bright lights.
7. Big cities usually have a lot of **traffic**, especially when people drive to work in the morning and drive home in the evening.
8. London is the **capital** of the United Kingdom. It is where the UK's government is.

a ___________ (n) the cars, trucks and other vehicles using a road
b ___________ (n) land that is not in towns or cities and may have farms and fields
c ___________ (adj) designed and made using the most recent ideas and methods
d ___________ (n) the number of people living in a place
e ___________ (n) damage caused to water, air and land by harmful materials or waste
f ___________ (n) the most important city in a country or state; where the government is
g ___________ (n) someone who has a lot of skill in or a lot of knowledge about something
h ___________ (n) a chance to do or experience something good

USING YOUR KNOWLEDGE

2 Read the title of the article. What do you think *mega* means?

a very busy   b very good   c very big

3 Read the article and check your answer.

Rise of the MEGACITIES

Megacity: a city with more than ten million people

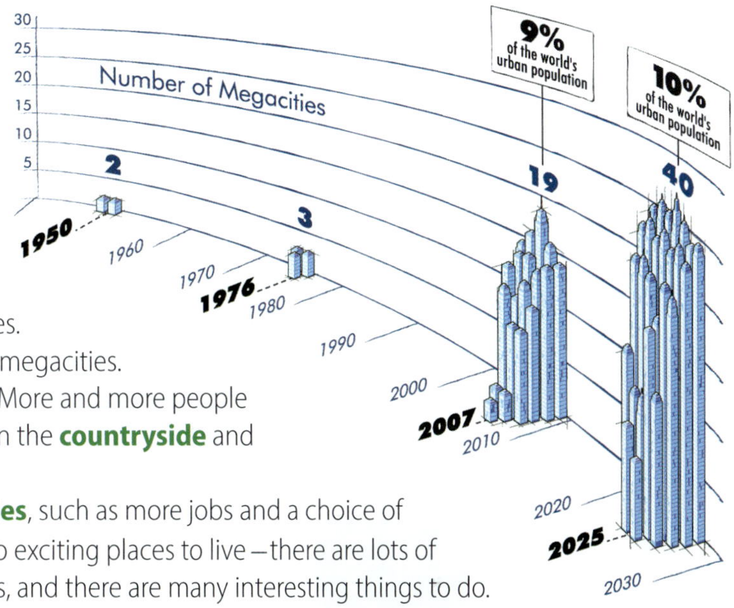

1 The number of megacities is growing very quickly. In the 1950s, there were only two megacities in the world.

2 Today, 12% of the world's urban[1] **population** lives in megacities. Studies show that there will be eight billion people in the world in 2025. **Experts** say that there will be 40 megacities.

3 Today, more than 35 cities in the world are megacities. 75% are in Asia, South America and Africa. More and more people around the world are leaving their homes in the **countryside** and moving to the city.

4 Many megacities have better **opportunities**, such as more jobs and a choice of schools and universities. Megacities are also exciting places to live – there are lots of different people, languages and restaurants, and there are many interesting things to do.

5 However, megacities have problems, too. The cities are very big and this can cause problems like **pollution** or poor housing[2].

Tokyo, Japan
37.8 MILLION

6 Tokyo is an exciting, **modern** city in the east of Japan. There are lots of jobs because most big companies in Japan are in Tokyo. It is also an excellent place to study – 20% of Japan's universities are in the city. However, Tokyo is very busy and the **traffic** is very bad. More than 8.7 million people use the trains every day.

Delhi, India
25 MILLION

7 Delhi is in the north of India. It has many beautiful monuments[3], interesting museums and modern restaurants. There is an exciting mix of different cultures in the city, and there are four official languages: Hindi, Urdu, Punjabi and English. However, there are not enough houses in some parts of Delhi. This means that many people live in large <u>slums</u> in the city.

Cairo, Egypt
18.3 MILLION

8 Cairo is the **capital** of Egypt and is the second-largest city in Africa. Cairo has important car and film industries. The city is the centre of many government offices and has many universities, one of which is over 1,200 years old.

[1]**urban** (adj) relating to towns and cities
[2]**housing** (n) places to live, such as apartments or houses
[3]**monuments** (n) old buildings or places that are important in history

WHILE READING

READING FOR MAIN IDEAS

4 Write *T* (true) or *F* (false) next to the statements. Then correct the false statements.

_____ **1** There are more megacities now than in 1950.

_____ **2** There are many opportunities to study in megacities.

_____ **3** Many people leave the countryside and move to a city.

_____ **4** Almost 35 cities in the world are megacities.

_____ **5** Most megacities are in Europe.

_____ **6** Finding a nice place to live is easy in megacities.

READING FOR DETAIL

5 Read the article again. Write the words from the box in the correct place in the table. Some words may fit in more than one place.

busy trains   good place to study   housing problem
important industries   interesting places to visit
lots of jobs   mix of different people   bad traffic

Tokyo	
Delhi	
Cairo	

SKILLS

Scanning for numbers

When scanning a text, look for specific information and details. They do not read the whole text. Readers often scan a text to find important numbers, percentages and dates.

SCANNING TO FIND INFORMATION

6 Find and circle all the numbers in the article.

7 Complete the student's notes with the correct numbers from the article.

1 number of megacities in 1950 = __________
2 predicted number of megacities in 2025 = __________
3 percentage of urban population in the world that live in megacities = __________ %
4 expected global population in 2025 = __________ billion
5 number of people who use the trains in Tokyo = __________ million
6 percentage of Japanese universities in Tokyo = __________ %
7 number of people living in Delhi = __________ million
8 number of official languages spoken in Delhi = __________
9 age of Cairo's oldest university = over __________ years old

READING BETWEEN THE LINES

WORKING OUT MEANING FROM CONTEXT

8 Look at the word *slums* underlined in the article. What do you think it means? Circle the correct answer.

a a very poor and crowded area in a city
b a very unclean house
c a very expensive area in the centre of a city

DISCUSSION

9 Work with a partner. Discuss the questions.

1 Are there any megacities in or near your country? Have you ever visited one? What did you think of it?
2 What are the advantages and disadvantages of living in the city?

PLUS

READING 2

PREPARING TO READ

UNDERSTANDING KEY VOCABULARY

1 Read the definitions. Complete the sentences with the words in bold.

> **area** (n) a region or part of a larger place, like a country or city
> **cheap** (adj) not expensive, or costs less than usual
> **city centre** (n) the main or central part of a city
> **expensive** (adj) costs a lot of money; not cheap
> **local** (adj) relating to a particular area, city or town
> **noisy** (adj) loud; makes a lot of noise
> **quiet** (adj) makes little or no noise

1 My hotel is ________ and calm. It is not in the busy part of the city, so it isn't loud at night.
2 Central Park is a nice ________ to visit in New York.
3 When people visit new cities, it's a good idea to ask ________ people for the best restaurants. They know the most about their city.
4 Since the airline was new, they offered ________ flights from Hong Kong to Bangkok. A lot of new customers bought tickets because of the low prices.
5 In Manchester, we took the bus to the ________ . That is where the main tourist sites in the city are located.
6 It's getting more ________ to live in big cities, so people who can't pay the high prices are moving away.
7 There was a lot of traffic on my street last night. It was too loud to sleep because of all the ________ cars.

PLUS

SCANNING TO PREDICT CONTENT

2 Read the title of the article on page 23. What general topic do you think the article is about?

a geography
b tourism
c history

3 Read the introduction and check your answer.

4 Circle the word or words in the introduction that tell you the answer.

HOMESTAY HOLIDAYS

A home away from home

1 Homestays are becoming more and more popular, and people around the world are offering their homes as hotels. Homestays offer **cheap** places to stay and the chance for guests to see the **area** like **local** people. They are very popular with students who want to stay in another country and learn a language. We asked three families who run homestays to tell us about where they live.

a ______________________________

The Atal family

2 Our family home is in the north of Nepal, in the Himalayan Mountains, in the village[1] of Manang. The village is small and very **quiet**. It is a very friendly place. The mountains are extremely beautiful. You can go for long walks and swim in the rivers, but there are no shops, cinemas or cafés.

b ______________________________

Kate and Julian Foxton

3 Our two-bedroom house is by the sea in the south-west of England. It is 15 minutes' drive to the nearest village of Portreath. There are lots of beaches, rivers and forests, and it is very quiet. We spend a lot of time reading books, watching films and going for walks. Our area is great for sports like surfing, kayaking and mountain biking. However, the houses here are expensive, which can be a problem for local people. There are no buses or trains here, so it can be difficult to get around without a car.

c ______________________________

Chafic and Aline Halwany

4 Our home is near the historic **city centre** of Beirut, Lebanon, a large city in the Middle East. There are lots of cafés and restaurants, which are open late at night. We love it here because it's so friendly and you can always find what you need. Lots of people come here to learn Arabic and French. There are also a lot of jobs and businesses here. However, it can be **noisy** at night and there is a lot of traffic during the day. The best thing about Beirut is the weather. It is nice all year round; it rains in the winter, but there is no snow.

[1]**village** (n) a very small town in the countryside

WHILE READING

READING FOR MAIN IDEAS

5 Write the headings above the matching paragraphs in the article.

A big city
A mountain village
A house near the forest

READING FOR DETAIL

6 Look at the summaries of the paragraphs. Cross out the incorrect words in bold and write the correct words. The first one has been done for you as an example.

1 The Atal family live in a ~~**city**~~ village. It is a **busy** place. The mountains are very **cold**.

2 Kate and Julian Foxton live in the **north** of England. The area is great for **theatres**. The houses are quite **cheap**.

3 Chafic and Aline Halwany live in a **small** city. People learn **English** and French in the city centre. There is a lot of traffic **at night**.

READING BETWEEN THE LINES

MAKING INFERENCES

7 Work with a partner. Discuss the questions.

1 Which families probably enjoy a quiet life?
2 Whose homestay might not be suitable for families with young children? Why not?

DISCUSSION

SYNTHESIZING

8 Work with a partner. Use ideas from Reading 1 and Reading 2 to answer the questions.

1 Why do people go to villages or to the countryside on holiday? What activities can people do in the countryside that they cannot do in the city?
2 What are the advantages and disadvantages of living in the countryside?
3 Why do young people leave the countryside to live in the city?
4 Think of a large city that you know. What do local people do for fun? What do people who visit the city on holiday do for fun? Do you think local people and tourists do the same things?

LANGUAGE DEVELOPMENT

NOUNS AND ADJECTIVES

GRAMMAR

A *noun* refers to a person, place or thing: girl, teacher, city, bus
An *adjective* describes a noun: tall, kind, busy, slow

noun		*adjective*	*adjective*	*noun*		*noun*	
Jenny	swam in the	**warm**	**blue**	**sea**	on her	**holiday**	last year.

1 Look at the sentence and the numbered words. Match the numbers to the parts of speech.

(1) Delhi has many (2) beautiful (1) monuments, (2) interesting (1) museums and (2) modern (1) restaurants.

noun ______ adjective ______

GRAMMAR

Adjectives

Adjectives describe nouns. Use the structure *adjective* + *noun*.

	adjective	*+ noun*
Beirut is an	**interesting**	**city**.
There are many	**excellent**	**restaurants**.

Adjectives also come after the verb *be*.
The city **is beautiful** in the summer.

Adjectives are never plural.
a different place → some ~~differents~~ places ✗ some different places ✓

2 Match the adjectives (1–5) to their opposites (a–e).

1 interesting	a expensive
2 cheap	b boring
3 polluted	c clean
4 beautiful	d quiet
5 noisy	e ugly

3 Complete the sentences with adjectives from Exercise 2.

1 There are lots of cars and traffic jams. The air is very ______ .
2 This is a(n) ______ city. Everything costs a lot of money.
3 My town is very ______ . There isn't any noise.
4 Edinburgh is a really ______ place. There are lots of things to do.
5 The building looks horrible. It's very ______ .

PLUS

GRAMMAR

Countable and uncountable nouns

Countable nouns are nouns that we can count.

one house → two houses

Uncountable nouns are nouns that we cannot count. Uncountable nouns often refer to food, liquids and ideas.

~~informations~~ ✗ information ✓

4 Look at the words in the box. Are they countable or uncountable nouns? Write them in the correct place in the table below. The first one in each column has been done for you as an example.

air beach building food hotel ~~house~~ ~~information~~ museum rain traffic transport village water work

countable nouns	uncountable nouns
house	information

GRAMMAR

Articles: *a*, *an* or zero article

Use *a* or *an* before a singular countable noun.

a house

Use *a* before a countable noun that starts with a consonant.

a cafe

Use *an* before a countable noun that starts with a vowel (*a*, *e*, *i*, *o*, *u*).

an area

Do not use *a* or *an* before a plural countable noun or an uncountable noun. This is the *zero article*.

buildings information

5 Complete the sentences with *a* or *an*. Write *X* for zero article.

1 They brought __________ bicycles to go to the mountains.
2 In a cinema, there is usually __________ sign for the exit.
3 I love to try different kinds of __________ food when I visit new cities.
4 You can easily take __________ train from Paris to Brussels.
5 I check my email in __________ internet café.
6 I usually travel with __________ friend.
7 Large cities often have __________ air pollution.

PLUS

QUANTIFIERS

GRAMMAR

Use a quantifier before a noun to describe the amount or number of something.

Some restaurants are closed today.

Use different quantifiers with countable and uncountable nouns.

quantifiers with countable nouns	quantifiers with uncountable nouns
a lot of / lots of *many* *some* *a few*	*a lot of / lots of* *some* *a little*

In negative sentences, use *many* with countable nouns and *much* with uncountable nouns.

My city doesn't have **many** tall buildings. My city doesn't have **much** traffic.

6 Write the quantifiers from the table above in the gaps. More than one option is possible.

a To talk about a large amount, we use ______________________

b To talk about a small amount, we use ______________________

7 Circle the correct words to complete the sentences.

1 Modern cities like Singapore have *a lot of / much* skyscrapers.
2 Small towns usually only have *a few / a little* shops and restaurants.
3 *A little / A lot of* cities have a famous football team.
4 *Many / Much* people live in Tokyo. It's one of the world's megacities.
5 Go online if you want *a few / some* information about things to do in the city.
6 My village doesn't have *many / much* public transport. We only have two buses each day!

8 Use phrases from columns A and B with quantifiers to write sentences that are true for you.

A	B
My town/city has	traffic at night.
We have	interesting people.
I have	neighbours.
My country has	megacities.

1 ______________________
2 ______________________
3 ______________________
4 ______________________

WRITING

CRITICAL THINKING

At the end of this unit, you will write six descriptive sentences. Look at this unit's writing task below.

> Describe the place where you live. Write about its positives and its negatives.

UNDERSTAND

EVALUATE

1 What are the main differences between the places described in Reading 1 and the places in Reading 2?

2 Read the section about living in a city (Beirut) from Reading 2 on page 23. Which features are positive (+) and which are negative (-)?

1 lots of cafés and restaurants ______
2 places stay open late at night ______
3 a lot of traffic ______
4 it can be noisy ______
5 a lot of jobs and businesses ______

SKILLS

Evaluating positives and negatives

Identifying and evaluating positive and negative features is very important. This can help you to understand arguments better and decide what you agree and disagree with. This skill is important in the classroom and in general life. Following this process can help you to form your opinion about something.

You can use a T-chart to write about positives (+) and negatives (–). Write about the positives in one column and the negatives in the other column.

3 Write the features from Exercise 2 in the correct place in the T-chart below.

positive (+)	negative (–)

4 Think of two more positives and two more negatives about living in a city. Write them in the T-chart in Exercise 3.

5 Complete a T-chart for one of the places in Reading 2. Add information you think might be true for that place. Look on the internet if you need more information. If you're not sure whether something is positive or negative, discuss with a partner.

positive (+)	negative (–)
beautiful	not many buses or trains

6 Share your T-chart with a group. Do you agree or disagree with each other? Explain your opinion.

APPLY

7 Think about where you live or where you are from. What are the positives and negatives about this place? Think about the things in the list below and create a T-chart like the one in Exercise 5.

- things to do
- jobs
- transport
- people
- houses

GRAMMAR FOR WRITING

SIMPLE SENTENCES 1

GRAMMAR

Subject + verb

A *simple sentence* is a complete thought that includes a subject and a verb. The subject of a sentence can be a noun or a noun phrase. A noun phrase is a group of words that acts like a noun. The verb can also be one word or a group of words.

subject (noun or noun phrase)	verb	
The people in the town	are	friendly.
The village	does not have	a shop.
My brother	lives	in the city.

Remember that a sentence is a *complete* thought.

✔ My brother lives in the city. (complete sentence)

✘ Lives in the city. (missing a subject)

✘ My brother in the city. (missing a verb)

1 Underline the subject and circle the verb in the sentences.

1 Paris is a beautiful city.
2 The town does not have a park.
3 I live in a small town.
4 Istanbul has many attractions.
5 Many students live in the city.
6 The village is not very exciting.
7 The shops are excellent.
8 The houses in the town are not very expensive.

2 Write simple sentences with the words. Write *S* next to the subject and *V* next to the verb in each sentence.

1 I / Mexican ______________________.
2 He / an engineer ______________________.
3 The people / nice ______________________.
4 We / happy ______________________.
5 Kyoto / beautiful ______________________.
6 It / a small town ______________________.

THERE IS / THERE ARE

GRAMMAR

Use *there is (not) / there are (not)* to explain what is in a place. These sentences do not use a subject.

There is a small beach with white sand.
There are many local cafés.

Contractions: *there's, there isn't, there aren't*

Use *there is (not)* to talk about one thing (singular) and *there are (not)* to talk about many things (plural).

	there is (not) / there are (not)	noun / noun phrase
singular	There is	a lake. / some traffic.
	There isn't	a cinema.
plural	There are	a lot of shops.
	There aren't	many beaches.

3 Circle the correct words to complete the sentences.

1 There *isn't / aren't* many traffic jams in my town.
2 There *is / are* an excellent museum.
3 There *isn't / aren't* people from many different countries.
4 There *is / are* a lot of apartments in the centre.
5 There *is / are* a beach.
6 There *isn't / aren't* many jobs.

4 Rewrite the sentences with the correct form of *there is (not) / there are (not)*.

1 Many restaurants are not in my town.
There aren't many restaurants in my town.
2 A famous museum is in my city.
____
3 A lake is not in my town.
____
4 A lot of cars are in my city.
____
5 Many expensive shops are in my city.
____
6 A few big hotels are in my town.
____
7 Many people are not in my town.
____

5 Work with a partner. Say whether your sentences in Exercise 4 are true for you.

6 Read the fact file about the city of Abu Dhabi in the United Arab Emirates. Then write one sentence for each item, using *there is (not) / there are (not)*.

Abu Dhabi, United Arab Emirates

- three sports stadiums
- a lot of museums
- many universities
- 11 ports
- one airport
- many five-star hotels
- a palace

1 There are three sports stadiums.
2 ______
3 ______
4 ______
5 ______
6 ______
7 ______

ACADEMIC WRITING SKILLS

CAPITAL LETTERS AND PUNCTUATION

SKILLS

Use a *capital letter* at the beginning of a sentence. Use a *full stop* (.) at the end of a sentence.

He lives in Abu Dhabi.

Use *commas* (,) to separate three or more items in a list.

Marta likes to read, exercise and play video games.

Use a capital letter with a *proper noun* (the name of a specific person, place or thing).

France Istanbul July Saturday

Always use a capital letter for *I*. I live in London.

1 Work with a partner. Correct the punctuation and capital letters in the paragraph.

PLUS

I
i live in montreal it is a city in canada it is a beautiful city there are many shops and restaurants the people are friendly there is an art festival in june people in montreal speak both french and english it is very crowded with tourists in the summer in the winter people like to ice skate cross-country ski and play ice hockey

WRITING TASK

Describe the place where you live. Write about its positives and its negatives.

PLAN

1 Look at the T-charts you made in the Critical thinking section. Choose three positives and three negatives that you are going to write about.

2 Refer to the Task checklist on page 34 as you prepare your sentences.

WRITE A FIRST DRAFT

3 Write three sentences describing positive features and three sentences describing negative features about where you live.

positive 1	
positive 2	
positive 3	
negative 1	
negative 2	
negative 3	

REVISE

4 Use the Task checklist to review your sentences for content and structure.

TASK CHECKLIST	✔
Did you write about the place where you live?	
Did you write six sentences?	
Are there three positive sentences?	
Are there three negative sentences?	

5 Make any necessary changes to your sentences.

EDIT

6 Use the Language checklist to edit your sentences for language errors.

LANGUAGE CHECKLIST	✔
Did you use nouns and adjectives correctly?	
Did you use countable and uncountable nouns correctly?	
Did you use articles correctly?	
Does every sentence have a subject and a verb?	
Did you use the correct form of *there is / there are*?	
Did you use capital letters, commas and full stops correctly?	

7 Make any necessary changes to your sentences.

OBJECTIVES REVIEW

1 Check your learning objectives for this unit. Write *3*, *2* or *1* for each objective.

3 = very well 2 = well 1 = not so well

I can …

watch and understand a video about Jakarta.	______
scan for numbers.	______
evaluate positives and negatives.	______
use nouns and adjectives.	______
identify and use countable and uncountable nouns.	______
use *a*, *an* and the zero article.	______
use quantifiers.	______
write simple sentences.	______
use *there is / there are*.	______
use capital letters and punctuation.	______
write descriptive sentences.	______

2 Use the *Unlock* Digital Workbook for more practice with this unit's learning objectives.

UNLOCK ONLINE

WORDLIST

area (n) ⊙	countryside (n) ⊙	opportunity (n)
beautiful (adj)	expensive (adj) ⊙	polluted (adj)
boring (adj)	expert (n) ⊙	pollution (n) ⊙
capital (n) ⊙	interesting (adj) ⊙	population (n) ⊙
cheap (adj) ⊙	local (adj) ⊙	quiet (adj)
city centre (n)	modern (adj)	traffic (n) ⊙
clean (adj) ⊙	noisy (adj) ⊙	ugly (adj)

⊙ = high-frequency words in the Cambridge Academic Corpus

LEARNING OBJECTIVES	IN THIS UNIT YOU WILL ...
Watch and listen	watch and understand a video about New Year celebrations in England and Scotland.
Reading skill	preview a text.
Critical thinking	identify important information.
Grammar	use prepositions of time and place; use adverbs of frequency; write simple sentences.
Academic writing skill	organize sentences into a paragraph.
Writing task	write a descriptive paragraph.

FESTIVALS AND CELEBRATIONS

UNIT 2

UNLOCK YOUR KNOWLEDGE

Work with a partner. Look at the photos and discuss the questions.

1 Where is the place in the large photo? What is happening in the photo?
2 What is happening in the small photos?
3 What countries do you think the photos are from?

PLUS

WATCH AND LISTEN

PREPARING TO WATCH

ACTIVATING YOUR KNOWLEDGE

1 Work with a partner. Look at the words in the box and read the glossary. Discuss the questions.

crowds of people	fireworks	midnight	parties	processions

1 Are each of the things in the box part of New Year's celebrations in your country? If yes, what happens exactly?
2 What do you know about New Year's celebrations in other countries?

PREDICTING CONTENT USING VISUALS

2 You are going to watch a video about New Year's celebrations in London, England and Edinburgh, Scotland. Work with your partner. Look at the pictures and describe what you can see in each one.

GLOSSARY

regret (v) to feel sorry about a situation, especially something that you did not do

media coverage (n) when a newspaper, television programme, etc. shows a particular thing happening

torch (n) a long stick with fire at the top of it, used as a light

procession (n) a long line of people, and sometimes cars and trucks, which moves forward slowly along the street, for example, during a festival

unique (adj) different from everyone and everything else

WHILE WATCHING

UNDERSTANDING MAIN IDEAS

3 ▶ Watch the video. Write *L* (London), *E* (Edinburgh) or *B* (both).

_____ 1 Crowds of people watch fireworks at midnight.
_____ 2 People wait a long time by the river.
_____ 3 People walk in a line through the city.
_____ 4 People come from all over the world.
_____ 5 The celebration is called Hogmanay.

UNDERSTANDING DETAIL

4 ▶ Watch again. Match each number (1–6) with what it describes in the video (a–f).

1 12,000 _____	**a** how long Hogmanay lasts
2 100,000 _____	**b** people in the procession in Edinburgh
3 three hours _____	**c** people watched by the River Thames
4 8,000 _____	**d** fireworks in London
5 five minutes _____	**e** how long the people waited in London
6 three days _____	**f** how long the fireworks lasted in Edinburgh

5 ▶ Watch again. Write *T* (true) or *F* (false) next to the statements. Correct the false statements.

_____ 1 It was a cloudy night in London.
_____ 2 The woman from Buenos Aires was pleased she came to London.
_____ 3 People in other countries could watch the London celebrations on TV.
_____ 4 In Edinburgh, people threw fireworks in the streets.
_____ 5 The Hogmanay festival is only celebrated in Scotland.

WORKING OUT MEANING FROM CONTEXT

6 Work with a partner. Discuss what the words in bold (1–3) mean.

'A time for **looking backwards**[1], **looking forwards**[2] and for **looking up**[3].'

DISCUSSION

7 Work in a small group. Discuss the questions.

1 Have you ever been part of a procession? If yes, when, why and what was it like?
2 Why do you think fireworks are popular for festivals and celebrations? Is it ever dangerous to have fireworks?
3 Do you think New Year is about looking backwards or forwards? Why?

READING

READING 1

UNDERSTANDING KEY VOCABULARY

PREPARING TO READ

1 Read the definitions. Complete the sentences with the words in bold.

> **celebrate** (v) to do something enjoyable because it is a special day
> **culture** (n) the habits, traditions and beliefs of a country or group of people
> **fireworks** (n) small objects which explode to make a loud noise and bright colours in the night sky
> **gift** (n) something that you give to someone, usually on a special day
> **lucky** (adj) having good things happen to you
> **traditional** (adj) following the ways of behaving or doing things that have continued in a group of people for a long time

1 People around the world usually __________ holidays and important events with a lot of food.
2 In Japan, guests usually give a small wrapped __________ , like cake or fruit, when they visit someone's home.
3 There are a lot of festivals in Korean __________ . Each one has special food and events.
4 For our International Day party, all of my classmates wore __________ clothes from their countries instead of their usual clothes.
5 In many countries, people believe the colour yellow is __________ . Wearing yellow will bring you good things, like joy and energy.
6 We are going to see the __________ tonight, because it is the last day of the holiday weekend. Children love to see the bright colours light up the sky.

SKILLS

Previewing a text

Before you read, look at the photos, title and subtitles. This gives you a lot of information about the topic of the text. If you know about the topic before you read, you will understand the text better.

PREVIEWING

2 Look at the photos, title and subtitles in the article. Circle the topic of the article.

a celebrations around the world
b weddings around the world
c games around the world

3 Read the article and check your answer.

Celebrate!

Piñatas

1 In Mexico, people often have piñatas at their parties. Parents put chocolates and other sweets inside the piñata and hang it on a tree. Children hit the piñata with a stick. It breaks and the sweets fall out onto the ground.

Noodles

2 In China, people **celebrate** weddings with an eight-course meal, because the word *eight* in Chinese sounds like the word for *good luck*. The last dish of the meal is always noodles. The noodles are long and thin. You have to eat them in one piece – you can't cut them. In Chinese **culture**, long noodles are **lucky**. Long noodles mean you will have a long life.

Mother's Day

3 Many people around the world honour their mothers on Mother's Day. In the UK, Mother's Day is celebrated in March or April. Sons and daughters like to give their mother a day to rest, so they might surprise her by cleaning the house or cooking a nice meal for her. They also give her **gifts** such as flowers or jewellery. Many families take their mother to a restaurant for lunch or dinner.

New Year's Eve

4 London celebrates New Year's Eve in a big way. Thousands of people go to the River Thames, and then, when it is dark outside, **fireworks** light up the sky and Big Ben, the bell in London's famous clock tower, chimes[1] at midnight. The next day, people eat a big meal with family and friends, go for a walk or just relax at home.

Coming of Age Day

5 In Japan, people celebrate Coming of Age Day, or *Seijin no hi*, on the second Monday in January. On this holiday, Japan congratulates people who have turned 20 years old between 2 April of the past year and 1 April of the current year. In Japanese culture, this is the age when teenagers become adults and take on[2] the responsibilities of being an adult. Young women usually wear a **traditional** *furisode* kimono, while young men often wear Western-style suits, and they attend a ceremony[3] in their area. They receive small presents and celebrate with their friends after the ceremony.

[1]**chimes** (v) makes a clear ringing sound
[2]**take on** (phr v) accept responsibility for something
[3]**ceremony** (n) a formal event that people go to, often for a holiday or to celebrate someone or something

WHILE READING

READING FOR MAIN IDEAS

4 Read the article again. Write the name of the country next to the description of the celebration.

1 use a stick to get sweets ____________
2 eat long noodles ____________
3 watch the fireworks ____________
4 wear traditional clothes ____________
5 give flowers or jewellery ____________

READING FOR DETAIL

5 Read the article again and write *T* (true) or *F* (false) next to the statements. Then correct the false statements.

_____ 1 Piñatas have flowers inside them.
____

_____ 2 Long noodles are unlucky in Chinese culture.
____

_____ 3 Mother's Day in the UK is in June or July.
____

_____ 4 On New Year's Day, some people eat with family and friends.
____

_____ 5 On Coming of Age Day, people wear special clothes.
____

READING BETWEEN THE LINES

RECOGNIZING TEXT TYPE

6 Where would you find this article? Circle the correct answer.

a in a magazine
b in an academic journal

7 Circle the features that helped you find the answer.

colour and design of the article   length of paragraphs   number of paragraphs   photos   title

DISCUSSION

8 Work with a partner. Discuss the questions.

1 What special days do you celebrate?
2 What do you do on these days?
3 What is your favourite celebration? Why?

READING 2

PREPARING TO READ

UNDERSTANDING KEY VOCABULARY

1 You are going to read about the Muscat Festival in Oman. Before you read, circle the best definition for the words or phrases in bold.

1 The children enjoyed a lot of **activities** at the party. They had their faces painted and played games.
   a things people do for fun
   b things people say
2 An important year in Russia's **history** is 1961, when they sent the first human into space.
   a events that are happening now
   b events that happened in the past
3 Food trucks are really **popular**. They are great for a tasty lunch.
   a liked by many people
   b not known by many people
4 The **highlight** of every holiday is getting together with loved ones.
   a location
   b most enjoyable part
5 Nearly everyone in town **takes part** in the race. There is a shorter race for children and a longer one for adults.
   a does an activity with other people
   b watches an event or competition
6 Thousands of **visitors** went to the museum on the first day it opened.
   a people who organize a party and invite guests
   b people who go to see a person or a place

PLUS

SKILLS

Proper nouns (e.g. names, countries, cities, days and months) begin with a capital letter. They can help when you are scanning a text because they are easy to see.

SCANNING TO PREDICT CONTENT

2 Read paragraph 1 in the text on page 44 and circle the proper nouns.

WHILE READING

READING FOR MAIN IDEAS

3 Read the text. Write the paragraph number (1–5) next to the ideas (a–e). Underline the information in the text that helped you find the answer.

a the countries people visit from Paragraph ____
b how long the Muscat Festival lasts Paragraph ____
c different events in the festival Paragraph ____
d international culture Paragraph ____
e the Tour of Oman Paragraph ____

Muscat Festival

1 One of the most important festivals in Oman is the Muscat Festival. The festival lasts for about one month and takes place in February every year. During the festival, many **activities** are available for people to **take part** in.

2 Large numbers of people, including local Omanis and **visitors** to Oman, go to the different events. The events are a celebration of both Omani and international **history** and traditions. The events happen in different places across the country. Many businesses show their products for people to look at and buy.

3 The Muscat Festival also includes the very **popular** six-day Tour of Oman cycle race. Professional cyclists from around the world take part in the race. The race is 1,000 kilometres long, and it takes the cyclists up the beautiful Jabal Al Akhdhar – the Green Mountain.

4 Other **highlights** of the Muscat Festival include the chance to try out different types of food at the Oman Food Festival. The Muscat Art Festival also offers Arabic music, concerts and plays, and other entertainment for the whole family. The Festival of Lights is one of the most popular events at the Muscat Festival.

5 The Muscat Festival is an international event, with people visiting from countries as far away as Brazil and Cuba. Visitors also arrive from Italy, India, Russia, South Korea, Spain, Tunisia and Turkey, as well as many other countries. They enjoy the amazing clothes, food and music. Some people just enjoy the mix of different cultures.

READING FOR DETAIL

4 Read the text again. Complete the sentences with information from the text.

1 The Muscat Festival happens in the month of ________ .
2 People from all over the world ________ the festival.
3 The English name for the Jabal Al Akhdhar is the ______________ .
4 You can see plays at the ______________ .
5 The Festival of Lights is a very ________ event.
6 Visitors enjoy clothes, ________ and ________ .

READING BETWEEN THE LINES

RECOGNIZING TEXT TYPE

5 Where would you find this text?

a in a guidebook on the culture of Oman
b in a textbook on the economy of Oman

6 What other topics would you expect to find in the book? Add two more topics to the list.

1 food
2 theatre
3 ________
4 ________

DISCUSSION

SYNTHESIZING

7 Work with a partner. Use ideas from Reading 1 and Reading 2 to answer the following questions.

1 Would you like to go to the Muscat Festival? Why / Why not?
2 Think about an interesting festival in your country. What information would you give a visitor? Answer the questions.
   a What is the festival?
   b When is it?
   c Where is it?
   d What happens?
3 Compare the celebrations you read about with other celebrations you know. How are they the same? How are they different?

PLUS

LANGUAGE DEVELOPMENT

PREPOSITIONS OF TIME AND PLACE

GRAMMAR

Use *on* with a specific date or day.
The holiday is **on** 1 May / **on** Saturday.

Use *in* with a month and with *the morning*, *the afternoon* and *the evening*.
Use *in* with a country, city or town.
The holiday **in** May.
We eat a special dinner **in** the evening.
I spend my holidays **in** Scotland / **in** Glasgow.

Use *at* with a specific time or with *night* and *the weekend*.
Use *at* with *school*, *college*, *university*, *work* and *home*.
We eat dinner **at** seven o'clock **at** night.
We learn a lot **at** school.

1 Write the words from the box in the correct place in the table.

a town eight o'clock home Istanbul June my country night school Sunday Thailand the evening the morning Tuesday work 1 January

	on	*in*	*at*
places			
times			

2 Complete the sentences with *on*, *in* or *at*.

1 People celebrate good news ________ work with their colleagues.
2 We are going to have a big family meal ________ Saturday.
3 The festival is ________ November.
4 My brother's anniversary is ________ 2 December.
5 The children wake up ________ seven o'clock.
6 People celebrate New Year ________ Australia.
7 We stay ________ home for the whole day.
8 We eat dinner late ________ night.
9 We meet our friends ________ the weekend.

PLUS

ADVERBS OF FREQUENCY

GRAMMAR

Use adverbs of frequency to talk about habits. They describe how often someone does something. Adverbs of frequency usually go before the verb in a sentence.

In Mexico, people **often** have piñatas at their parties.
In China, my family **always** celebrate weddings with an eight-course meal.
Children in the UK **sometimes** clean the house on Mother's Day.
Young Japanese women **usually** wear traditional clothing on their Coming of Age Day.
People **never** cut their noodles at weddings in China.

0% — 100%

never — sometimes — often — usually — always

3 Complete the sentences with adverbs of frequency. Write sentences that are true for you.

1 I __________ visit my parents in the holidays.
2 I __________ visit my mother on Mother's Day.
3 I __________ celebrate New Year.
4 I __________ go to weddings.
5 I __________ eat sweets on special occasions.

4 Work with a partner. Compare and discuss your answers. What is the same and what is different?

5 Put the words in order to make complete sentences.

1 in the evening / usually starts / The dinner / eight o'clock / at / .

____

2 chocolates / festivals / at / always eat / I / .

____

3 to call / She / forgets / never / her family / .

____

4 sometimes get / toys / money instead of / The children / .

____

5 our winter holiday / We / skiing / often go / for / .

____

PLUS

WRITING

CRITICAL THINKING

At the end of this unit, you will write a descriptive paragraph. Look at this unit's writing task below.

Describe a festival or special event.

SKILLS

Identifying important information

Before you write, you need to decide what information is important to your topic. One way to do this is by categorizing information. One way to categorize information is with an ideas map.

APPLY

1 Complete the ideas map with information from Reading 2 on page 44.

1 Write the name of the event in the centre of the ideas map.
2 Write about the topics in the list below in the correct part of the ideas map.
- when the event is
- where the event is
- what people eat and drink at the event
- what people do at the event
- what people wear to the event

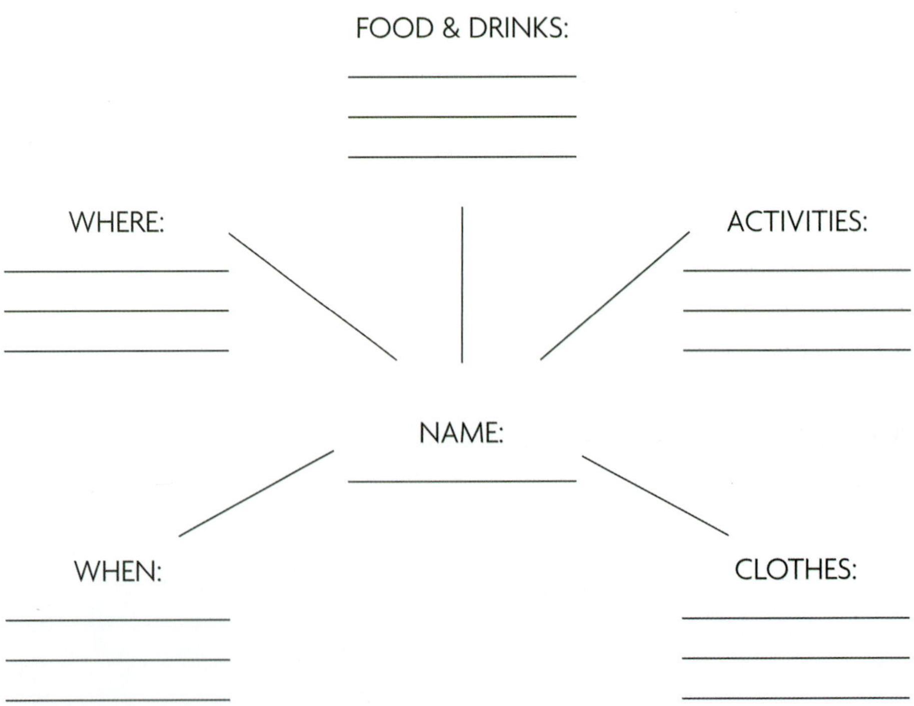

2 Compare your ideas map with a partner. Did you include the same information? Add and change your information if necessary.

ANALYZE

3 Work with a partner. Think about any festivals or celebrations that you both know about. Discuss them with your partner and choose one to write about.

CREATE

4 Complete the ideas map with information about the festival or celebration you chose in Exercise 3. You will use this to brainstorm ideas for your writing task.

FOOD & DRINKS: ___ ___ ___

WHERE: ___ ___ ___

ACTIVITIES: ___ ___ ___

NAME: ___

WHEN: ___ ___ ___

CLOTHES: ___ ___ ___

5 Look at your ideas map. Do any topics need more information? Ask other students in your class or look on the internet to find more information.

GRAMMAR FOR WRITING

SIMPLE SENTENCES 2

GRAMMAR

Objects and extra information

A simple sentence needs to have a *subject* and a *verb*. The verb comes after the subject.
After the verb, there can be an *object* (usually a *noun* or *noun phrase*). You can also add extra information by using an *adjective* or a *prepositional phrase*.

subject	verb	noun phrase
I	visit	my family.

subject	verb	adjective
The people	are	happy.

subject	verb	prepositional phrase
The festival	is	in May.

1 Underline the subject and circle the verb in each sentence.

1 The children wear traditional clothes.
2 My family and I watch the fireworks.
3 I visit my aunt and uncle.
4 People in the UK celebrate university graduation.
5 My parents and I go to the city centre.

2 Underline the words that come after the verb in each sentence. Then write *N* for noun, *A* for adjective, and *P* for prepositional phrase.

1 My family eat at home. ______
2 The costumes are beautiful. ______
3 We exchange presents. ______
4 I celebrate in the evening. ______
5 The festival is traditional. ______

3 Put the words in order to make complete sentences.

1 celebrate / People in Wales / New Year / .

____

2 at the weekend / My parents and I / cook together / .

____

3 excited / is / Everyone in my town / about the festival / .

____

4 eat / My family / in the morning / .

____

5 do not visit / my grandparents / We / .

____

GRAMMAR

Prepositional phrases

Sometimes a sentence can have an object and a prepositional phrase. The prepositional phrase comes after the object.

noun phrase (subject)	verb	noun phrase (object)	prepositional phrase
People in Mexico	eat	a special meal	in the evening.

The prepositional phrase can also come at the beginning of the sentence, followed by a comma.

prepositional phrase	noun phrase (subject)	verb	noun phrase (object)
In the evening,	people in Mexico	eat	a special meal.

4 Underline the prepositional phrase in each sentence. Circle the object.

1 We watch films at night.
2 In India, people celebrate the Magh Bihu festival.
3 People clean their homes in the morning.
4 Children have parties at school.
5 On Saturday, we will watch the parade.

ACADEMIC WRITING SKILLS

ORGANIZING SENTENCES INTO A PARAGRAPH

SKILLS

In written English, sentences are organized into paragraphs. A paragraph is a group of sentences about the same topic. A new topic should be put in a new paragraph.

A paragraph has a *topic sentence*, *supporting sentences* and a *concluding sentence*. A paragraph is often written in this order:

1 The **topic sentence** describes what the paragraph is about. It is usually the first sentence in a paragraph.
2 The **supporting sentences** tell more about the topic and give details and examples. They are in the middle of the paragraph.
3 The **concluding sentence** ends the paragraph. It usually summarizes the main idea in the paragraph. The concluding sentence often starts with phrases like *In conclusion*, *In summary* or *To summarize*. Some short paragraphs do not have a concluding sentence.

1 Look at the sentences. They are from two different paragraphs. Paragraph 1 is about a city. Paragraph 2 is about a festival. Organize the sentences into two paragraphs. Write *1* or *2* next to each sentence.

a Janadriyah is a cultural festival in Saudi Arabia. 2
b It is a very noisy city. 1
c People watch the camel-racing event. ____
d In the summer, it is very hot. ____
e It happens in February or March. ____
f I live in Taipei. ____
g There are lots of shops and restaurants. ____
h People listen to traditional poetry. ____
i It's a great place to live. ____

2 Read the paragraph and follow the steps.

1 Circle the topic sentence and write *T* next to it.
2 Underline the supporting sentences and write *S* next to them.
3 Highlight the concluding sentence and write *C* next to it.

When I was a child, my classmates and I always celebrated International Teacher's Day. It was my favourite day of the year. We brought gifts for our teacher. We ate special food and we usually played games. The teachers loved Teacher's Day and the students loved it, too. To summarize, I have very special memories of Teacher's Day.

3 Read the sentences. Write *T* next to the topic sentence, *S* next to the supporting sentences and *C* next to the concluding sentence.

a Holi usually lasts for two days and people laugh, have fun and forget their troubles. ______

b Holi is an ancient festival that celebrates the beginning of spring. ______

c India celebrates the Festival of Colours, also known as Holi. ______

d In conclusion, this festival is an interesting Indian celebration. ______

e During this festival, friends and family get together and throw coloured water and powder at each other – this activity celebrates the beautiful colours that come with spring. ______

4 Read the supporting sentences again. Circle the details and examples in the sentences that tell you more about the topic.

5 Look again at Organizing sentences into a paragraph on page 52. Write the sentences about Holi in the correct order.

____

____

____

____

____

PLUS

WRITING TASK

Describe a festival or special event.

PLAN

1 Look at the ideas map below. Use the information to complete the model paragraph below.

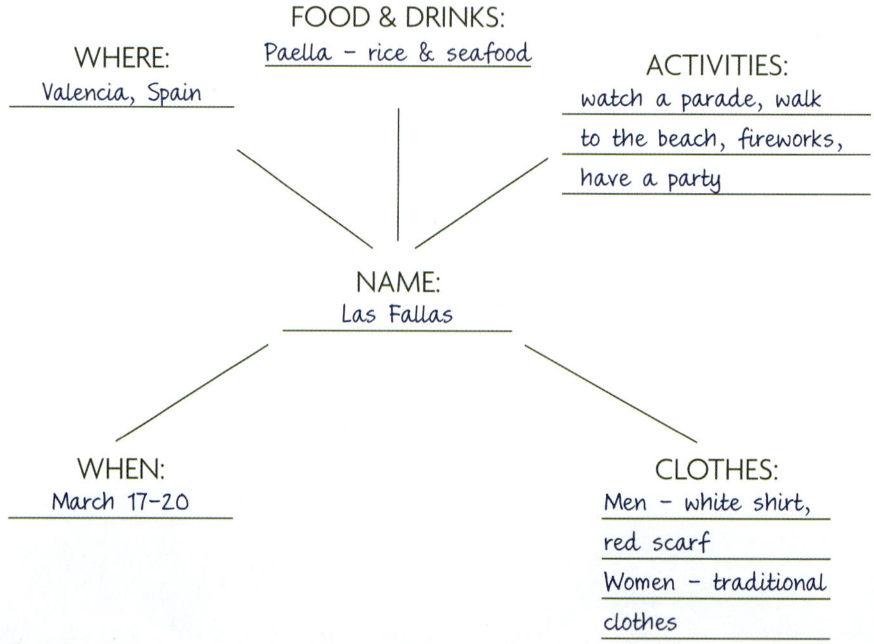

In Valencia, Spain, people celebrate Las Fallas. Las Fallas is in the month of (1)__________ every year. It starts on the (2)__________ and ends on the 20th. People watch a (3)__________ in the streets. In the evening, everyone walks to the (4)__________ and has a party. There are fireworks. People also eat (5)__________ . It is a meal of (6)__________ and seafood. Men wear a white shirt and a (7)__________ scarf, and women wear traditional (8)__________ . In conclusion, Las Fallas is an enjoyable festival in Spain with fun activities, great food and interesting traditional clothing.

2 Look back at the ideas map you completed for Exercise 4 in the Critical thinking section. Use your notes to write a topic sentence in the paragraph planner below. Write about the name of the event you chose and where it takes place.

topic sentence: name and place	
supporting sentence (1): when	
supporting sentence (2): activities	
supporting sentence (3): food and drinks	
supporting sentence (4): clothes	
concluding sentence	

3 Use your notes to write four supporting sentences about the details of the festival (when it takes place, activities, food and drinks, and clothes) in the planner.

4 Write your concluding sentence in the planner. Your concluding sentence should summarize the main idea of the paragraph.

5 Refer to the Task checklist on page 56 as you prepare your paragraph.

WRITE A FIRST DRAFT

6 Use the sentences in the paragraph planner to write a paragraph.

REVISE

7 Use the Task checklist to review your paragraph for content and structure.

TASK CHECKLIST	✔
Did you describe a festival or special event?	
Are the sentences organized in a paragraph?	
Does the paragraph start with a topic sentence stating the name of the event and where people celebrate it?	
Does the paragraph say when the event is?	
Does the paragraph have supporting sentences about the activities, food and drink, and clothes?	
Does the paragraph have a concluding sentence?	

8 Make any necessary changes to your paragraph.

EDIT

9 Use the Language checklist to edit your paragraph for language errors.

LANGUAGE CHECKLIST	✔
Did you use *on*, *in* and *at* correctly?	
Did you use adverbs of frequency correctly?	
Did you use correct sentence structure?	
Did you use prepositional phrases correctly?	

10 Make any necessary changes to your paragraph.

OBJECTIVES REVIEW

1 Check your learning objectives for this unit. Write *3*, *2* or *1* for each objective.

3 = very well 2 = well 1 = not so well

I can …

watch and understand a video about New Year celebrations in England and Scotland.	____
preview a text.	____
identify important information.	____
use prepositions of time and place.	____
use adverbs of frequency.	____
write simple sentences.	____
organize sentences into a paragraph.	____
write a descriptive paragraph.	____

2 Use the *Unlock* Digital Workbook for more practice with this unit's learning objectives.

UNLOCK ONLINE

WORDLIST

activity (n) ⊙	gift (n) ⊙	popular (adj) ⊙
celebrate (v)	highlight (n) ⊙	take part (phr v)
culture (n) ⊙	history (n) ⊙	traditional (adj) ⊙
fireworks (n)	lucky (adj)	visitor (n)

⊙ = high-frequency words in the Cambridge Academic Corpus

LEARNING OBJECTIVES	IN THIS UNIT YOU WILL ...
Watch and listen	watch and understand a video about advertising.
Reading skills	read for main ideas; make inferences.
Critical thinking	identify appropriate answers.
Grammar	give opinions; connect ideas.
Academic writing skill	write topic sentences.
Writing task	write a one-sided opinion paragraph.

THE INTERNET AND TECHNOLOGY

UNIT 3

UNLOCK YOUR KNOWLEDGE

Look at the photo and answer the questions.

1 What do you think the woman's job is?
2 What is she using the tablet for?
3 How much time do you spend on the internet every week?
4 What activities do you use the internet for?

WATCH AND LISTEN

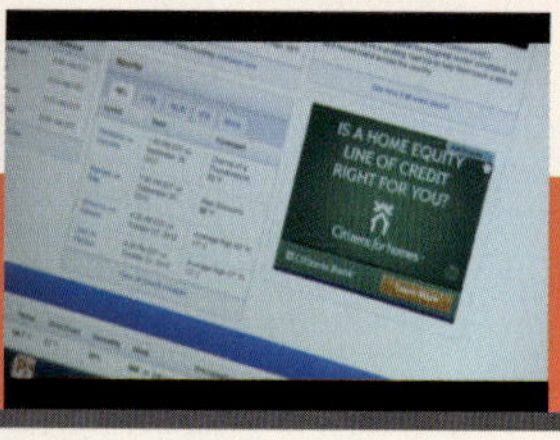

PREPARING TO WATCH

ACTIVATING YOUR KNOWLEDGE

1 Work with a partner and answer the questions.

1 Why do people buy things from websites?
2 What kinds of adverts do you see online?
3 Do you ever worry when you use technology? Why / Why not?

USING YOUR KNOWLEDGE

2 Read the opinion. Do you agree or disagree? Discuss your answer with your partner.

> People should never give personal information on websites when they are online in public places such as airports, hotels or coffee shops.

GLOSSARY

habit (n) something that you do regularly, almost without thinking about it

advertising (n) the business of trying to persuade people to buy products or services

ad (n) an advert: a picture, short video, song, etc. that tries to get you to buy a product or service

predict (v) to say what you think will happen in the future

clue (n) a sign or piece of information that helps you solve a problem or answer a question

WHILE WATCHING

UNDERSTANDING DETAIL

3 Watch the video. Complete each sentence with a word from the box.

looking	showing	taking	talking	texting	walking

1 A woman is ________ someone on her phone.
2 A man is ________ to someone on his phone.
3 People are ________ while ________ at their phones.
4 A woman is ________ a photo with her camera.
5 A computer is ________ an advert on a website.

4 Watch again. Circle the correct answers.

1 The amount of data is growing by 2.5 *million* / *billion* gigabytes every day.
2 All that data is worth a lot of *money* / *time*.
3 Mike Baker decided to help change the world of *travelling* / *advertising*.
4 Companies could predict what people might want to *buy* / *sell*.
5 Mike's program looks at data *quickly* / *slowly*.
6 Personalized adverts are sent to *companies* / *customers*.

UNDERSTANDING MAIN IDEAS

5 Match the sentence halves. Compare your answers with a partner.

1 The amount of data is growing because ____
2 Using data is difficult because ____
3 Mike Baker found a partner because ____
4 Mike hunts data because ____

a he needed help.
b there is too much of it.
c we leave information every time we call, text or search online.
d it is worth a lot of money.

MAKING INFERENCES

6 Work with a partner. The speaker in the video says, 'Maybe it's better to see ads for things you like than for things you don't care about.' What does he mean?

DISCUSSION

7 Work in small groups. Discuss the questions.

1 What are some differences between adverts online, on TV and in newspapers or magazines?
2 What kinds of adverts do you prefer to see on your phone or computer?
3 Name five companies that advertise around the world. Describe one advert that you remember.

READING

READING 1

PREPARING TO READ

UNDERSTANDING KEY VOCABULARY

1 Read the sentences (1–7) and write the words in bold next to the definitions (a–h).

1 People should always use a **secret** password on their smartphone. This helps to keep their information safe.
2 After I buy the correct **software**, I'll be able to make music and draw pictures on my computer.
3 Sarah has an **interest** in the newest technology, so she always learns about it very quickly.
4 The software allows teachers to **collect** information about how well their students are doing.
5 Shopping websites must have strong **security**. People have to be sure their personal information and credit card numbers are safe.
6 Ahmed likes to **record** his friends when they do something funny. Then he shares the videos online.
7 After I saw an online **advert** for a new smartphone, I really wanted to get one.
8 Many people don't want to pay to use news websites because so much of the news is already **free** online.

a __________ (n) a picture, short film, etc. that tells people about something they can buy
b __________ (n) something you enjoy doing or learning about
c __________ (v) to get things from different places and bring them together
d __________ (adj) costing no money
e __________ (n) the things that are done to keep someone or something safe
f __________ (v) to store sounds, pictures or information on a camera or computer so that they can be used in the future
g __________ (n) programs you use to control what a computer does
h __________ (adj) not known or seen by other people

SCANNING TO PREDICT CONTENT

2 Before you read, circle the title and subtitle in the website on page 63.

3 Circle the best description of the topic of the website.

a the benefits (+) of the internet
b the dangers (–) of the internet
c why people use the internet

4 Read the website and check your answers.

TECH EXPERT TODAY HOME NEWS REVIEWS SHOP

Someone's always watching you online …

How companies buy and sell your personal information

1 Did you know that when you surf the web, websites in some countries put **secret software** on your computer? The software **collects** a large amount of information about you and sends it to internet companies. The internet companies sell it to other businesses. Your personal information can also be gathered from social media sites. There are many ways your information can be used.

2 First, companies collect your information and **record** all your online habits. They find out where you live, what websites you visit and what you do online. With this information, they can guess other things about you. For example, they can guess if you are male[1] or female[2], how old you are and your **interests**. The companies use this information to decide which **adverts** are best for you. Two people can go to the same website, but they will see different adverts. For example, someone who likes sports could see an advert for trainers, and someone who likes films might see an advert for a film.

3 Your personal information could also be sold. Some companies collect information just so they can sell it to other businesses. A business that collects and sells personal information is called a *data broker*. When data brokers sell your information, a lot of different companies will know your online habits. Then these companies will advertise products or other websites to you.

4 Another way your personal information can be collected is through social media. When your information is on social media, a lot of people can see it. Even if you don't use social media, a friend might post a picture or video of you with your name on it. Pictures and videos can be shared for **free** on social media, which is one of the great advantages. However, that same act of sharing could be a problem for your own **security**. If someone knows too much about you, they can steal your identity. Then they can buy things online and post messages while pretending to be you.

5 However, it's not all bad news. The law is finally changing when it comes to technology. In the European Union, for example, they have introduced the General Data Protection Regulation (GDPR). This rule means that internet users can now ask companies to show them what information they have about them and even make them delete it. If other countries do the same, the internet could soon be a much safer place.

find out more

[1]**male** (adj) a man
[2]**female** (adj) a woman

THE NEXT STEP

FREE
WEB HOSTING
FOR ONE YEAR
SIGN UP TODAY!

LAPTOPS
at low prices

Career placement
We'll get you working!

Download free ringtones, apps and wallpaper for your smartphone!

WHILE READING

SKILLS

Reading for main ideas

When reading, it is important to understand the main ideas in the text. Remember that each paragraph has one topic. The main idea of a paragraph is the most important point of what the author says about the topic. The main idea can often be found in the topic sentence, which is usually the first or second sentence in the paragraph. Because the main idea connects all of the information together, reading for main ideas is the key to understanding the text.

READING FOR MAIN IDEAS

5 Read the text again. Circle the correct ending for each sentence.

1 In some countries, internet companies *ask you for information / take information without asking you.*

2 Internet companies show *different adverts to different people / the same adverts to everyone.*

READING FOR DETAIL

6 Write the words from the box in the correct place in the table. For some items, more than one answer is possible.

a data broker   other websites you might like   the websites you visit
your address   your age   your gender (male/female)   your interests
your online habits   your social media page

A What do internet companies find out about you?	B What do internet companies guess about you?	C What do internet companies decide?	D How do internet companies find out about you?

READING BETWEEN THE LINES

SKILLS

Making inferences

When people read, they often make inferences about a text. To make an inference, think about what the author writes, the way they write it and what you already know about the subject. Make a guess about information that isn't in the text. Inferences are not facts, so different answers are often possible.

MAKING INFERENCES

7 Look at the adverts on the website on page 63. What can you guess about the people using the website? Answer these questions.

1 How old are the users?
2 What are the users' interests?

8 What can you infer from the text? Circle the correct answers.

a You don't usually know what websites are collecting information about you.
b You should be careful with your personal information when you travel.
c Someone could pretend to be you and send an email to your friend.
d Data brokers probably make a lot of money selling personal information.

9 Work with a partner. Compare and discuss your answers.

DISCUSSION

10 Read the three opinions about the topic of the website. Circle the opinion you agree with most.

a I don't think companies should take any of this information from you – it's really bad. Think about the danger of so many people knowing your private information.

b I don't see the problem. Companies need to make money somehow – we get a lot of free things on the internet, and this is a good way to pay for them. There are benefits for everyone.

c I think it's great. If companies can show you adverts for things you like, you can find out about new things.

11 Work with a partner. Compare and discuss your answers.

READING 2

PREPARING TO READ

UNDERSTANDING KEY VOCABULARY

1 Read the definitions. Complete the sentences with the words in bold.

> **affect** (v) to influence someone or something; to cause change
> **creative** (adj) good at thinking of new ideas or creating new and unusual things
> **download** (v) to copy programs, music or other information electronically from the internet to your device (e.g. a computer)
> **educational** (adj) providing or relating to teaching and learning
> **imagination** (n) the part of your mind that creates ideas or pictures of things that are not real or that you have not seen
> **improve** (v) to get better or to make something better

1 There are a lot of apps you can __________ onto your phone to help you learn a new language.
2 I like to watch __________ videos so I can learn something new. I just watched one about the history of aeroplanes.
3 Gabriela took a course to __________ her computer skills. Now she can type faster and find information on the internet more easily.
4 Reading, telling stories and having new adventures can help children to develop their __________ .
5 Art students are very __________ . On my course, we use new software to make some really interesting and beautiful designs.
6 Spending too much time on your smartphone may __________ your health in negative ways. It can hurt your eyes and give you a headache.

PLUS

2 Write the words from the box in the correct place in the table.

> advantage disadvantage benefit negative positive

+	–

3 Do you know any other words that could go in the table? If you do, add them.

USING YOUR KNOWLEDGE

4 You are going to read about video games. Before you read, discuss the questions with a partner.

1 Why do some people like video games?
2 What ages do you think most video game players are?

Video games for kids: win or lose?

1 Do video games **affect** our children negatively? Today, our children spend more and more time online. Many children spend a lot of their free time playing games on the internet, on video game systems or on their mobile devices. In the UK, 99% of kids aged 8 to 15 play video games every week, and children as young as five play video games regularly. This information tells us that the benefits and dangers of video games must be carefully considered.

2 For many people, video games are fun and **educational**. They have bright lights, funny cartoons[1] and exciting stories. Everywhere you look, you can see children playing these games. They play on buses and trains, in restaurants and even at school. Video games also make you think in a **creative** way and you have to move your hands and eyes quickly. This can **improve** the way that a child's brain works. Video games also make children use their **imagination**. The player has to do many creative things, like draw, tell stories and build things. Video games are also a good way to teach children about technology because they can learn how computers and other devices work while they play.

3 However, a recent study suggests that video games can also be bad for children. First, children can **download** many games for free. They don't need money, so they don't need to ask their parents if they can download the games. This means that parents often don't know if their children are playing violent or scary games. Second, many children spend too much time playing games on computers, smartphones and tablets and this can lead to health problems – children who spend too much time on the computer and don't exercise can become overweight[2]. Third, if children spend too much time playing games instead of doing homework, they can have problems at school and get bad grades. Finally, video games can affect children's social skills. Playing and working with friends is very important for children and it teaches them how to talk to other people. If children spend too much time playing video games by themselves, they might not learn how to play with their friends.

4 In conclusion, it seems clear that video games have some advantages and some disadvantages. On the one hand, they are fun and have many educational benefits for children. On the other hand, they can cause problems with children's health and social skills. It is up to parents to know what games their children are playing and how much time they spend on them. Parents should also make sure their children get enough exercise and spend time with other children.

[1]**cartoons** (n) films made using characters that are drawn and not real
[2]**overweight** (adj) too heavy or weighing more than the usual amount

WHILE READING

READING FOR MAIN IDEAS

5 Read the text on page 67. Write the paragraph numbers that include the main ideas below. Then write the sentences from the text that contain each main idea.

1 Video games have some disadvantages. Paragraph: _____
Sentence: ______________________________

2 Video games have some advantages. Paragraph: _____
Sentence: ______________________________

READING FOR DETAIL

6 Cross out the advantages and disadvantages in the table that are not mentioned in the text.

+	–
Video games ...	Video games ...
1 are creative.	6 can cause health problems.
2 improve the way children think.	7 are boring.
3 teach children about money.	8 can make it difficult for children to learn to talk to people.
4 are fun.	9 can be unsuitable for children.
5 can help children exercise.	10 can cause problems between parents and children.

7 Work with a partner. Discuss whether you agree with the advantages and disadvantages in Exercise 6.

READING BETWEEN THE LINES

RECOGNIZING TEXT TYPE

8 Read the questions. Circle the correct answer. Compare your answers with a partner.

1 What type of text is this?
  a an essay
  b a newspaper article
  c a website

2 Who do you think is the author?
  a a parent
  b a journalist
  c a student

DISCUSSION

SYNTHESIZING

9 Work with a partner. Use ideas from Reading 1 and Reading 2 to answer the following questions.

1 How much time do you spend on the internet each week? Do you think it is too much? Would older people agree with your answer? Why / Why not?

2 What are some of your online habits? What might an internet company learn about you from your online habits?

PLUS

LANGUAGE DEVELOPMENT

COMPOUND NOUNS

VOCABULARY

In English, you can put two or more words together to form a new word. This is called a *compound noun*. Compound nouns are very common in English. Some compound nouns are written as one word (e.g. keyboard = key + board). Others are written as two or three separate words (e.g. computer program).

A **laptop** is a small computer that you can carry around with you.
A **touch screen** is a screen on a computer, smartphone or tablet that you touch in order to give it instructions.
A **password** is a secret word that allows you to use your computer.
A **home page** is the first page you see when you look at the internet.

1 Match the compound nouns (1–6) to their definitions (a–f).

1 video game
2 computer program
3 keyboard
4 email address
5 website
6 smartphone

a a set of pages of information on the internet
b a set of keys on a computer that you use to type
c a mobile phone that can be used as a computer
d a game that is played on a screen
e instructions that make a computer do something
f an address for an email inbox

PLUS

2 Use the compound nouns from Exercise 1 to complete the sentences.

1 My computer's ______________ is broken. I can only type in capital letters.
2 I just bought a new ______________ . I can use the internet anywhere now.
3 What's your ______________ ? I'll send you the pictures from the party.
4 I found a(n) ______________ with good information I can use for my essay.
5 I can play this ______________ on my computer or on my smartphone. It's really fun!
6 I downloaded a(n) ______________ to check my computer for viruses.

GIVING OPINIONS

GRAMMAR

Use phrases such as *I think that*, *I believe that*, *It seems to me that* and *In my opinion* to talk about your opinion.

Opinion: *Video games are bad for children.*

I think that video games are bad for children.
I believe that video games are bad for children.
It seems to me that video games are bad for children.
In my opinion, video games are bad for children.

3 Look at the phrases for giving opinions. Which phrase needs a comma at the end of it?

a I think that
b I believe that
c It seems to me that
d In my opinion

4 Complete the sentences with an adjective. Write sentences that are true for you.

1 Video games are ___________ .
2 Online shopping is ___________ .
3 Social media sites are ___________ .
4 Online banking is ___________ .
5 Smartphones are ___________ .
6 Watching videos online is ___________ .

PLUS

5 Rewrite the sentences in Exercise 4 to show that they are your opinion. Use phrases from the box above.

1 ______________________________
2 ______________________________
3 ______________________________
4 ______________________________
5 ______________________________
6 ______________________________

6 Share your sentences from Exercise 5 with a partner. Give reasons. Do you have the same or different opinions?

WRITING

CRITICAL THINKING

At the end of this unit, you will write a one-sided opinion paragraph. Look at this unit's writing task below.

The internet wastes our time. It does not help us do more work. Do you agree or disagree?

SKILLS

Identifying appropriate answers

When you answer a question, it is important to include only information that is related to the topic. You need to understand exactly what the question asks you to do and how you have to do it. You can then decide which information to include and how to appropriately answer the question.

ANALYZE

1 Match each question to the correct way to answer it.

1 How does the internet waste our time? How does it help us do more work? ______

2 The internet wastes our time more than it helps us do work. Do you agree or disagree? ______

a Give your opinion about whether the internet wastes our time or helps us do more work. Give examples to support your argument.

b Describe the ways the internet wastes our time and the ways it helps us do more work.

2 Read what the three students think about the internet. What advantages and disadvantages do they talk about?

The internet is great for being able to read newspapers from all over the world. I can read news from back home in China. Also, when I read a newspaper in English, I learn new words. If I just want to have fun, I can play a few video games. However, I have to be careful about how much time I spend on the internet because I don't want to get addicted to it.

Chen

Sometimes I like to do my homework at home, instead of going to the library. The internet is useful for that. I can go to a lot of different websites for help with my homework, and I can email my classmates and teachers if I have questions. Sometimes I worry, though. I have so much information on my computer that if it breaks, I'll lose a lot of it.

Adalaide

I love social media sites because I can connect with people who like the same music that I do. And without social media, I wouldn't learn about all the films that are made in different countries and which ones I should go and see. Of course, the internet is a great place for learning, too. I watch a lot of educational videos and I learn interesting things about cultures and traditions that are different from mine.

Yasir

3 Work with a partner. Discuss whether you agree with the students' opinions. Explain your reasons.

APPLY

4 Look at the students' opinions again. Decide whether you think they are advantages or disadvantages of using the internet. Then write them in the correct column of the table.

The internet helps us do work.	The internet wastes our time.

5 Add two more points to each column.

EVALUATE

6 Work with a partner. Which points are the most convincing? Why?

GRAMMAR FOR WRITING

CONNECTING IDEAS

GRAMMAR

and, also and *too*

Use the conjunction *and* or the adverbs *also* or *too* to add information. Connecting ideas makes your writing better and easier to understand.

Use *and* to join two ideas in a single sentence.

My sister has a computer. She has a smartphone.
→ My sister has a computer **and** a smartphone.

Jessica texts her friends. She shares photos.
→ Jessica texts her friends **and** shares photos.

You can use *also* and *too* to connect the ideas in two separate sentences.

My sister uses her computer a lot. She **also** has a smartphone.
My sister uses her computer a lot. She has a smartphone, **too**.

Put *also* before the main verb. Put *too* at the end of the sentence. *Too* usually has a comma before it.

1 Join each pair of sentences to make one simple sentence with *and*.

1 Video games are boring. They are bad for children.
Video games are boring and bad for children.

2 You can share photos. You can talk to your friends.

3 I use online banking. I check my email.

4 She does homework on her computer. She watches films on her computer.

5 I often shop for clothes on the internet. I pay with my credit card.

2 Look at the sentence pairs. Rewrite the sentences with *also* or *too* in the second sentence to connect the ideas.

1 Many people download music. They download videos. (also)

2 I write a blog about travelling. I read a lot of travel blogs. (too)

3 I read the newspapers online. I check social media. (also)

4 I look at maps on my phone. I look at photos on my phone. (also)

GRAMMAR

Compound sentences

A *compound sentence* contains two independent clauses (clauses which have their own subject and verb). Use a conjunction, such as *and* or *but*, to link two independent clauses.

Use *and* to add information.

Lina doesn't have a smartphone. She doesn't want one.
→ Lina doesn't have a smartphone, **and** she doesn't want one.

Use *but* to give contrasting or different information or ideas.

Martin reads books on a tablet. Jose likes to read printed books.
→ Martin reads books on a tablet, **but** Jose likes to read printed books.

Use a comma before *and* or *but* in a compound sentence.

3 Join each pair of simple sentences to make one compound sentence. Use *and* or *but*.

1 Video games are boring. They can affect your social skills.
Video games are boring, and they can affect your social skills.

2 I sent an email to Alan. He did not write back to me.

3 I like to shop online. My father thinks it's not safe.

4 I call my mother every Saturday. I visit her every Sunday.

5 I bought a new phone. It doesn't work.

6 You can check the weather. You can find a good restaurant.

7 Some games are educational. Other games are just for fun.

8 I want to learn about the new company. I can't find their website.

9 The class went to the library. They learnt how to use the new computers.

10 The home page gives the company's address. It is the wrong address.

GRAMMAR

However

You can also connect two sentences with contrasting or different information or ideas with *however*.

Smartphones are very popular. They are very expensive.
→ Smartphones are very popular. **However,** they are very expensive.

Use *however* at the start of a new sentence, followed by a comma.

4 Rewrite each pair of sentences. First write a compound sentence using *but*. Then link the ideas with *however*.

1 The internet is very useful. It can be dangerous.
   a The internet is very useful, but it can be dangerous.
   b The internet is very useful. However, it can be dangerous.

2 Many apps are educational. Some apps are a waste of time.
   a ______________________
   b ______________________

3 I use online banking. I sometimes forget my password.
   a ______________________
   b ______________________

4 I use the internet on my smartphone. Sometimes it is very slow.
   a ______________________
   b ______________________

5 Work with a partner. Look at Exercise 4. Discuss whether you think sentences 1 and 2 are true.

ACADEMIC WRITING SKILLS

TOPIC SENTENCES

SKILLS

A topic sentence tells you the main idea of a paragraph. It is usually the first or second sentence in a paragraph. A topic sentence has two parts: the *topic* and the *controlling idea*. The topic tells you what the paragraph is about. The controlling idea gives the topic a focus.

topic — *controlling idea*

The internet has many advantages. You can find information quickly and keep in touch with your friends. It's also easy to share photos and watch videos. The internet makes life easier.

1 Look at paragraphs 2 and 3 in Reading 2 on page 67. Underline the topic sentences.

2 Read the topic sentences. Underline the topic. Circle the controlling idea.

1 Social media sites make it easy to keep in touch with your friends.
2 Smartphones can be expensive.
3 Information on the internet is not reliable.
4 You can access information online from all over the world.

3 In each paragraph, the topic sentence is missing. Write the topic sentences from Exercise 2 above the correct paragraph.

a ______________________________

It is easy to spend a lot of money on them. Contracts for the phones can also cost a lot of money. It is important to be careful and pay attention to what you spend.

b ______________________________

You can read newspapers, magazines and blogs from many different countries. You can even translate information from other languages, using a translation website. It is easy to find out what is happening anywhere you want.

c ______________________________

You can look at your friends' photos and see what they are doing. Your friends can send you messages and links. You can also share interesting articles and videos.

d ______________________________

Anyone can publish articles and information online. Websites often do not say who wrote an article or where they got their facts. People can write things that are not true.

PLUS

WRITING TASK

The internet wastes our time. It does not help us do more work. Do you agree or disagree?

PLAN

1 Look at the question above. Do you agree or disagree? Circle the answer that is true for you.

1 2 3 4

1 = strongly disagree
2 = disagree more than agree
3 = agree more than disagree
4 = strongly agree

2 Look at the table in Exercise 4 of the Critical thinking section. Highlight the three ideas that best support your opinion.

3 Look at the paragraph planner.

1 Write your topic sentence in the planner.
2 Write your three supporting ideas in the planner.

topic sentence:	supporting idea 1:
	supporting idea 2:
	supporting idea 3:

4 Refer to the Task checklist on page 78 as you prepare your paragraph.

WRITE A FIRST DRAFT

5 Write the first draft of your paragraph. Connect your ideas and sentences.

REVISE

6 Use the Task checklist to review your paragraph for content and structure.

TASK CHECKLIST	✔
Did you answer the question correctly?	
Did you include a topic sentence with a controlling idea?	
Did you give your opinion on the topic?	
Did you include three supporting ideas?	
Did you include a concluding sentence?	

7 Make any necessary changes to your paragraph.

EDIT

8 Use the Language checklist to edit your paragraph for language errors.

LANGUAGE CHECKLIST	✔
Did you use compound nouns correctly?	
Did you use the correct sentence order with the phrases *I think that*, *I believe that*, *it seems to me that* and *in my opinion*?	
Did you use *and*, *also* and *too* correctly?	
Did you use *but* and *however* correctly?	
Did you use compound sentences?	

9 Make any necessary changes to your paragraph.

OBJECTIVES REVIEW

1 Check your learning objectives for this unit. Write *3*, *2* or *1* for each objective.

3 = very well 2 = well 1 = not so well

I can …

watch and understand a video about advertising.	_____
read for main ideas.	_____
make inferences.	_____
identify appropriate answers.	_____
give opinions.	_____
connect ideas.	_____
write topic sentences.	_____
write a one-sided opinion paragraph.	_____

2 Use the *Unlock* Digital Workbook for more practice with this unit's learning objectives.

UNLOCK ONLINE

WORDLIST

advert (n)	email address (n)	secret (adj) ʘ
affect (v) ʘ	free (adj) ʘ	security (n) ʘ
collect (v) ʘ	imagination (n) ʘ	smartphone (n)
computer program (n)	improve (v) ʘ	software (n) ʘ
creative (adj) ʘ	interest (n) ʘ	video game (n)
download (v)	keyboard (n)	website (n) ʘ
educational (adj) ʘ	record (v) ʘ	

ʘ = high-frequency words in the Cambridge Academic Corpus

LEARNING OBJECTIVES	IN THIS UNIT YOU WILL ...
Watch and listen	watch and understand a video about tornadoes.
Reading skills	read for detail; use your knowledge to predict content.
Critical thinking	analyze graphs.
Grammar	use comparative and superlative adjectives.
Academic writing skills	write topic sentences for descriptive paragraphs about a graph; write supporting sentences; give examples with *like*, *such as* and *for example*.
Writing task	write a paragraph describing data from graphs.

WEATHER AND CLIMATE

UNIT 4

UNLOCK YOUR KNOWLEDGE

1 Match the types of weather in the box to the small photos.

rain (n)	snow (n)	sun (n)	wind (n)

2 What is your favourite type of weather? Why?

3 What is your least favourite type of weather? Why?

4 Look at the large photo. What type of weather do you see?

PLUS

WATCH AND LISTEN

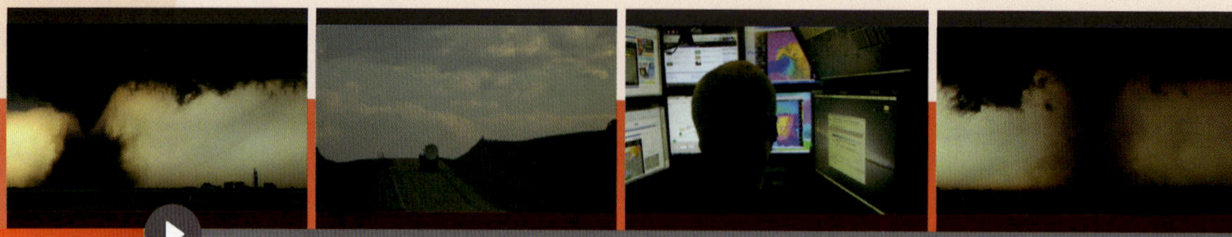

PREPARING TO WATCH

ACTIVATING YOUR KNOWLEDGE

1 Work with a partner and answer the questions.

1 What is a thunderstorm?
2 Why are some people afraid of thunderstorms?
3 How can wind from a storm be dangerous?

PREDICTING CONTENT USING VISUALS

2 Look at the pictures from the video. Discuss the questions with your partner.

1 What do you think the video is about?
2 Where do you think it takes place?
3 What do you think is the man's job?

GLOSSARY

extreme (adj) the worst or most serious, for example, extreme weather conditions
tornado (n) an extremely strong, dangerous wind that blows in a circle
alley (n) a narrow street between buildings
produce (v) to cause a reaction or a result
Doppler radar (n) a special radar system that can give us information about a storm
spin (v) if something spins, it turns around and around quickly

WHILE WATCHING

UNDERSTANDING DETAIL

3 Watch the video. Circle the correct answers.

1 The middle of the United States is called Tornado *Alley* / *Valley*.
2 The year *2010* / *2011* was very bad for tornadoes.
3 That year a dangerous tornado killed more than *160* / *60* people.
4 Scientists *can* / *cannot* predict when and where tornadoes will happen.
5 Josh Wurman is a *computer* / *weather* scientist.
6 *Seventy-five* / *Twenty-five* percent of thunderstorms produce tornadoes.
7 Finding the right thunderstorm is *easy* / *difficult*.

4 Watch again. Match the questions (1–5) to the correct answers (a–e).

1 What does spring bring?	a Tornadoes.
2 What killed people in Joplin, Missouri?	b Warm, wet air.
3 What is Josh Wurman studying?	c A dangerous tornado.
4 What does Josh use to find storms?	d Tornadoes happen quickly.
5 Why did the team have to move fast?	e A Doppler radar scanner.

UNDERSTANDING MAIN IDEAS

5 Read the statements. What is the video mainly about? Circle the best answer.

a Some thunderstorms produce tornadoes, but others do not.
b Tornadoes are one of the most dangerous kinds of weather in the world.
c The winds in a tornado can spin faster than the winds in a hurricane.

MAKING INFERENCES

6 Work with a partner. Do Josh and his team enjoy their work? How do you know?

DISCUSSION

7 Work with a partner. Discuss the questions.

1 Is Josh Wurman's job important? Why / Why not?
2 What other jobs are related to weather?
3 Why do people choose to live in areas with extreme weather?

8 Work in small groups. Make a list of five things you would do to prepare for a tornado.

READING

READING 1

PREPARING TO READ

UNDERSTANDING KEY VOCABULARY

1 You are going to read a text about extreme weather. Before you read, look at the definitions. Complete the sentences with the words in bold.

> **almost** (adv) not everything, but very close to it
> **cover** (v) to lie on the surface of something
> **dangerous** (adj) can harm or hurt someone or something
> **huge** (adj) extremely large in size or amount
> **last** (v) to continue for a period of time
> **lightning** (n) a flash of bright light in the sky during a storm
> **thunder** (n) the sudden loud noise that comes after a flash of lightning

1 I think the big snow storm will ________ the ground in snow. We won't be able to see any grass at all.
2 Although ________ can be very scary, it is also beautiful when it flashes in the sky.
3 ________ every house on our street was damaged by the storm. Only two houses were OK.
4 Asli got sick when the weather changed. Luckily, it didn't ________ long. She felt better after a couple of days.
5 The ________ scared our cats. They hate the loud noise.
6 There has been a ________ increase in rainfall this year. As a result, the lakes and rivers are at the highest levels in years.
7 Swimming in the rain can be ________ if there is lightning. You should get out of the water right away so you don't get hurt.

USING YOUR KNOWLEDGE

2 Work with a partner and discuss the questions.

1 What kind of weather do you have where you live? Is it different throughout the year? If so, how?
2 What does the word *extreme* mean?
3 What is an example of extreme weather?

1 Extreme weather

Extreme weather is when the weather is very different from normal. Extreme weather can happen over an hour, a day or a long period of time. It can be **dangerous** and, in some cases, it can cause natural disasters[1].

2 Hurricanes

A hurricane is a type of storm. These storms are also called cyclones or typhoons. In North America and Central America, they are called hurricanes; in the North Pacific, they are called typhoons; and in the Indian Ocean and South Pacific, they are called cyclones. These storms are **huge** – they can be over 500 kilometres wide. They start over the ocean and move towards land. When they come to land, they bring **thunder**, **lightning**, strong winds and very heavy rain. They can be very dangerous and destroy buildings and even kill people.

3 Heat waves and droughts

A heat wave is when there are high temperatures and it is much hotter than normal. In many areas, heat waves are not a problem. However, in parts of Australia, temperatures may reach 48 °C in a heat wave, and **last** for a few days or even months. And in some places, such as parts of eastern Australia, heat waves can cause droughts[2]. In a drought, there is not enough water for farmers to grow food. In some cases, people die because they don't have enough water to drink. Droughts are common in many countries in Africa, but in the last ten years, droughts have also happened in Afghanistan, China and Iran.

4 Rainstorms

Too much rain can cause floods[3]. Floods can destroy buildings and kill people. They can also destroy plants and food, which can mean that there is not enough food for people to eat. In 2015, there were very bad floods in South America. In Argentina, the Paraguay River was **almost** 15 metres higher than normal and water **covered** the streets. In Paraguay, hundreds of thousands of people had to leave their homes. Strong winds damaged the power lines, and several people died. It was the worst flood in 50 years.

5 Sandstorms

A sandstorm is a large storm of dust and sand with strong winds. Sandstorms can be very dangerous. It is difficult to travel by car because people can't see anything. Even walking can be difficult. Sandstorms are common in the Middle East and in China. One of the worst sandstorms was in Iraq in 2011 when a storm lasted a whole week, causing many people to have breathing problems.

[1]**disasters** (n) events that cause a lot of harm or damage
[2]**droughts** (n) long periods when there is no rain and people do not have enough water
[3]**floods** (n) if a place floods or is flooded, it becomes covered in water

WHILE READING

READING FOR MAIN IDEAS

3 Read the text on page 85. Then circle the statement (a or b) that contains the most important idea in each paragraph (1–5).

1 Paragraph 1
 a Extreme weather is unusual and can cause natural disasters.
 b Extreme weather can happen over a short time or a long time.
2 Paragraph 2
 a Hurricanes cover a very wide area.
 b Hurricanes are huge, dangerous storms.
3 Paragraph 3
 a In a heat wave, temperatures are hotter than normal.
 b Heat waves sometimes occur in Australia.
4 Paragraph 4
 a In 2015, there were floods in South America.
 b Floods happen when there is too much rain.
5 Paragraph 5
 a A sandstorm is a storm with a lot of wind and dust.
 b Certain countries have frequent sandstorms.

SKILLS

Reading for detail

When reading a text, it is important to understand the details as well as the main ideas. Details give specific information about the main ideas. You can find details in a text by looking for key words. Read the sentences with the key words carefully to understand important information.

READING FOR DETAIL

4 Circle the correct ending (a or b) for each sentence (1–4).

1 Hurricanes move from …
 a land to sea.
 b sea to land.
2 Heat waves …
 a may lead to droughts.
 b aren't usually a big problem.
3 Paraguay had …
 a a very big flood in 2015.
 b no food for people to eat in 2015.
4 In 2011, …
 a China had a bad sandstorm.
 b Iraq had a bad sandstorm.

READING BETWEEN THE LINES

RECOGNIZING TEXT TYPE

5 Circle the correct answer. Identify the parts in the text that helped you answer each question.

1 What type of text is this?
 a an excerpt from a newspaper b an excerpt from a textbook
2 Who would be interested in reading this text?
 a someone studying Biology b someone studying climate
3 What kind of information is included in the text?
 a facts b opinions

DISCUSSION

6 Discuss the questions with a partner.

1 What is the worst weather you have ever experienced?
2 Has the weather in your country changed in recent years?

READING 2

PREPARING TO READ

SKILLS

Using your knowledge to predict content

You can understand something better if you connect it to what you already know. Before you read something, first think about what you already know about the topic. This gets you ready for reading and helps you understand.

USING YOUR KNOWLEDGE

1 You are going to read about the Sahara Desert. Before you read, try to answer the questions.

1 Where is the Sahara Desert?
 a South Africa
 b North Africa
 c Central Asia

2 What is the weather like there?
 a hot and dry
 b cold and wet
 c hot and wet

UNDERSTANDING KEY VOCABULARY

2 Read the sentences (1–6). Write the words in bold next to the definitions (a–f).

1 It was hot and sunny all day, so it was a **shock** when it suddenly started to rain.
2 The temperature will **rise** over the summer months.
3 Let's wait and see what the weather is like tomorrow. Then we'll **decide** if we want to go to the beach or to a museum.
4 Be **careful** when you drive on icy roads. Go slowly and watch out for other cars.
5 Mawsynram, India has the most **precipitation** in the world. It gets about 11.9 metres of rain every year.
6 The temperature might **drop**, so we'll build a fire to stay warm.

a __________ (adj) paying attention to what you do so that you don't have an accident, make a mistake or damage something
b __________ (v) to decrease; to fall or go down
c __________ (v) to choose between one possibility or another
d __________ (n) a big, unpleasant surprise
e __________ (v) to increase; to go up
f __________ (n) rain or snow that falls to the ground

PLUS

3 Read the article on page 89 and check your answers to Exercise 1.

WHILE READING

READING FOR MAIN IDEAS

4 Write the paragraph number (1–8) next to the best title (a–e). You do not need to use all the paragraph numbers.

a Stay out of the sun ______
b Drink water ______
c Stay cool during the day and warm at night ______
d Don't eat too much ______
e Stay with your car ______

READING FOR DETAIL

5 Match the sentence halves. Use the graph on page 89 and information in paragraph 2 to help you.

1 The coldest time is	a between 2 pm and 4 pm.
2 The average amount of rain in a year	b is –1 °C.
3 The temperature is 33 °C	c is 70 mm.
4 The coldest temperature at night	d at four o'clock in the morning.

READING BETWEEN THE LINES

RECOGNIZING TEXT TYPE

6 Where might you find an article like this?

a in a newspaper
b in a travel magazine
c in a Maths textbook

DISCUSSION

7 Look at the list. Which things would you need most if you were alone in the desert? Choose the three most important things.

a a blanket
b a mirror
c 20 litres of water
d a radio
e a map
f a hat

8 Work with a partner. Compare your answers and explain your choices.

SYNTHESIZING

9 Work with a partner. Choose three extreme weather situations from Reading 1 and Reading 2. Discuss some survival tips for the extreme weather you chose.

PLUS

SURVIVING[1] THE SEA OF SAND

How to stay alive in the Sahara Desert

Brad Rogers

1 Can you imagine a sea of sand three times bigger than India? This is the Sahara Desert, the largest desert in the world. It covers 11 countries in North Africa and is over 9 million square kilometres. That's more than 25% of Africa.

2 In the Sahara, temperatures are very different during the day and at night. It is much hotter during the day than at night. During the day, the hottest time is between 2 pm and 4 pm, when temperatures **rise** to 33 °C. But it is very cold at night – the coldest time is at 4 am, when temperatures fall to –1 °C. The Sahara is very dry. The average **precipitation** in a year is only 70 millimetres.

3 Because of the extreme temperatures in the desert, it is a very difficult place to survive. Marco Rivera, our survival expert, has some tips.

4 Take warm clothes and a blanket. You will need a hat, long trousers and a woollen jumper to keep you warm at night. During the day, cover your body, head and face. Clothes protect you from the sun and keep water in your body. You will also need a warm blanket at night. It can get cold very quickly. When the temperature **drops**, it can be a **shock** and make you feel even colder.

5 A car is easier to see than a person walking in the desert. You can also use the mirrors from your car to signal[2] to planes and other cars. You can use your car tyres to make a fire. A fire is easy to see. It will help people find you and it will keep you warm at night.

6 Try to drink some water at least once every hour. You need your water to last as long as possible. Drink only what you need. When you talk, you lose water from your body. Keep your mouth closed and do not talk.

7 If you eat, you will get thirsty and drink all of your water more quickly. You can eat a little, but only to stop you from feeling very hungry. Eat very small amounts of food and eat very slowly. You can live for three weeks with no food, but you can only live for three days without water.

8 It is very important to stay out of the sun during the day. Make a hole under your car and lie there. This will keep you cool and help you sleep. Find a warm place to sleep at night. A small place near a tree or a rock will be the warmest. But be **careful** before you **decide** where to sleep. Dangerous animals like snakes and scorpions also like to sleep in these places. Look carefully for animals before you lie down.

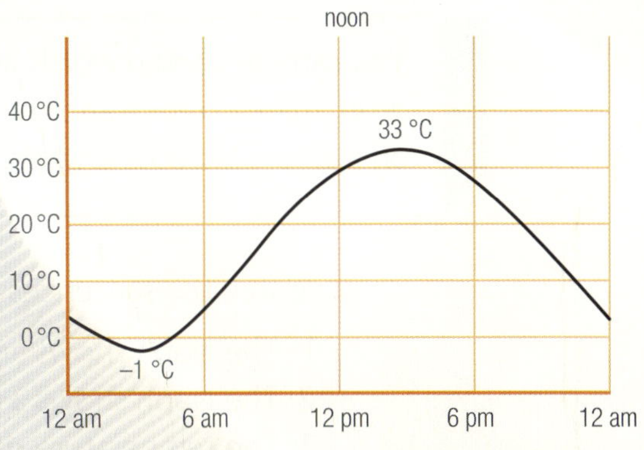

[1]**surviving** (v) staying alive in dangerous situations
[2]**signal** (v) make a sign or wave to get someone's attention

LANGUAGE DEVELOPMENT

COLLOCATIONS WITH *TEMPERATURE*

A

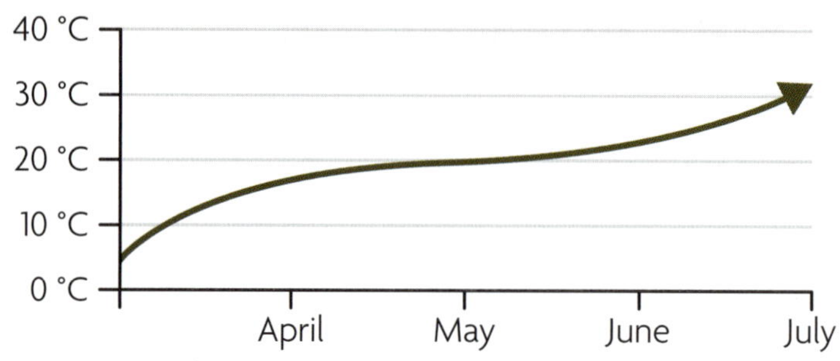

B

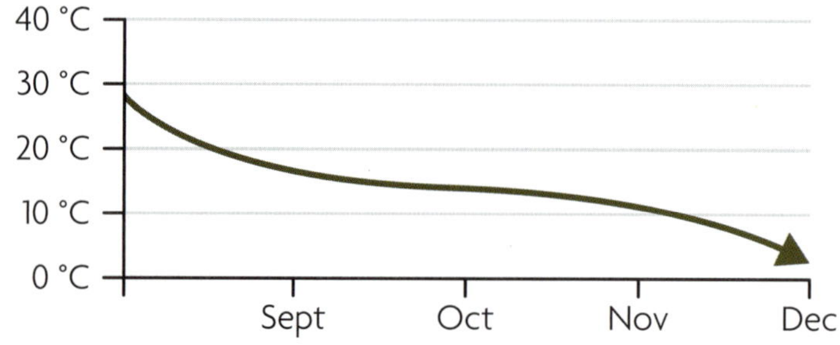

1 Look at the graphs (A and B). Circle the correct word to complete the sentences (1–4) about the graphs.

1 In July, there are *high* / *low* temperatures.
2 In December, there are *high* / *low* temperatures.
3 The *maximum* / *minimum* temperature is 32 °C in July.
4 The *maximum* / *minimum* temperature is 1 °C in December.

PLUS

DESCRIBING A GRAPH

VOCABULARY

You can use certain words and phrases to talk about graphs. Use the verbs *rise*, *drop*, *fall* and *reach* and the nouns *increase* and *decrease* to describe changes on a graph. *Increase* and *decrease* are also verbs.

2 Match the sentences (1–6) to the correct graph (A or B).

1 The graph shows an **increase** in temperature. ______
2 The graph shows a **decrease** in temperature. ______
3 The temperature **rises** to 32 °C. ______
4 The temperature **drops** to 1 °C. ______
5 The temperature **falls** to 1 °C. ______
6 The temperature **reaches** 32 °C. ______

3 Complete the statements with the bold words in Exercise 2.

1 Use ____________ and ____________ to talk about an increase in temperature.

2 Use ____________ and ____________ to talk about a decrease in temperature.

4 Look at the graphs (1–4). Circle the correct word to complete the sentences (a–b).

1
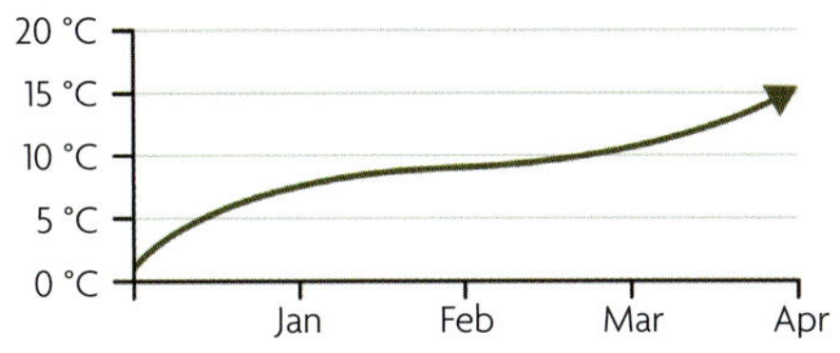

a The graph shows *an increase / a decrease* in temperature.
b In April, the temperature *reaches / falls* to 15 °C.

2
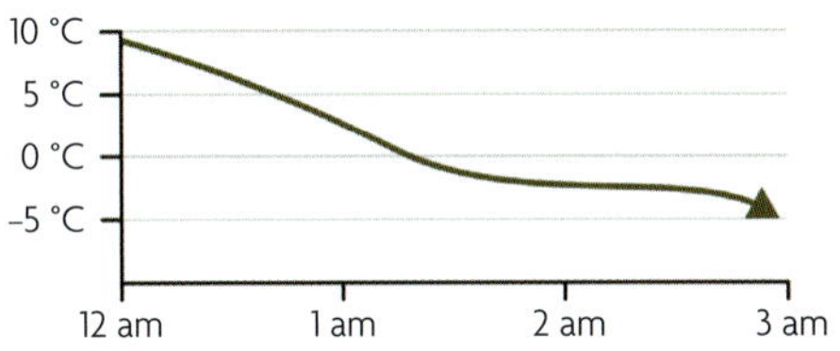

a The graph shows *an increase / a decrease* in temperature.
b At three o'clock, the temperature *drops / rises* to about –5 °C.

3
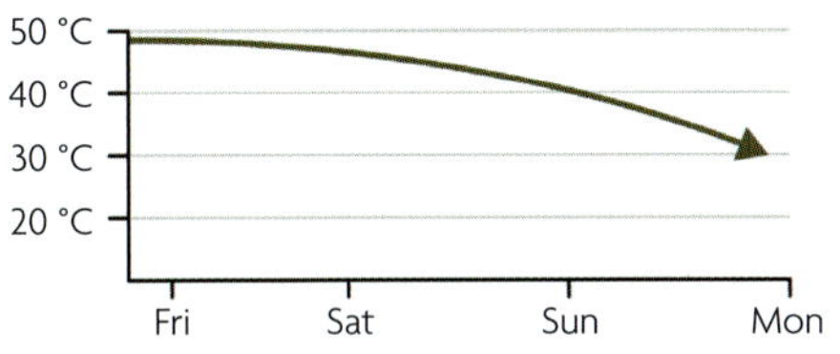

a The graph shows *an increase / a decrease* in temperature.
b On Monday, the temperature *reaches / falls* to 30 °C.

4
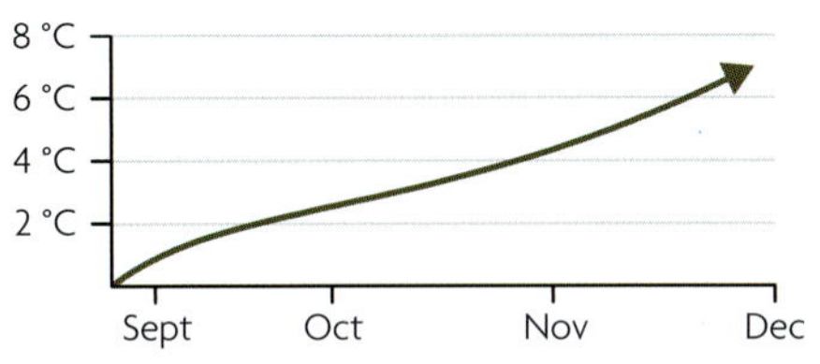

a The graph shows *an increase / a decrease* in temperature.
b In December, the temperature *rises / falls* to 7 °C.

PLUS

WRITING

CRITICAL THINKING

At the end of this unit, you will write a paragraph describing data from graphs. Look at this unit's writing task below.

Compare the weather in two places, using information from graphs.

SKILLS

Analyzing graphs

You can use graphs to show numbers or data. When you look at a graph, you can see the most interesting information quickly and easily. When you write about graphs, look at the highest and lowest numbers and then choose the most interesting information to write about.

UNDERSTAND

1 Look back at the graph in Reading 2 on page 89 and answer the questions.

1 What do the numbers on the left side of the graph show?
2 What do the numbers at the bottom of the graph show?
3 What does the highest point in the graph show?
4 What does the lowest point in the graph show?

ANALYZE

2 Look at the graphs (A–D). What kind of information does each one show? Check your answers with a partner.

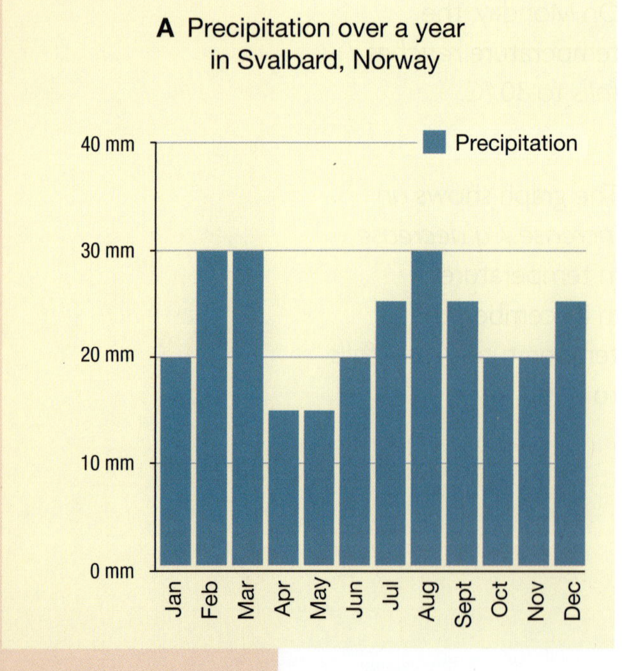

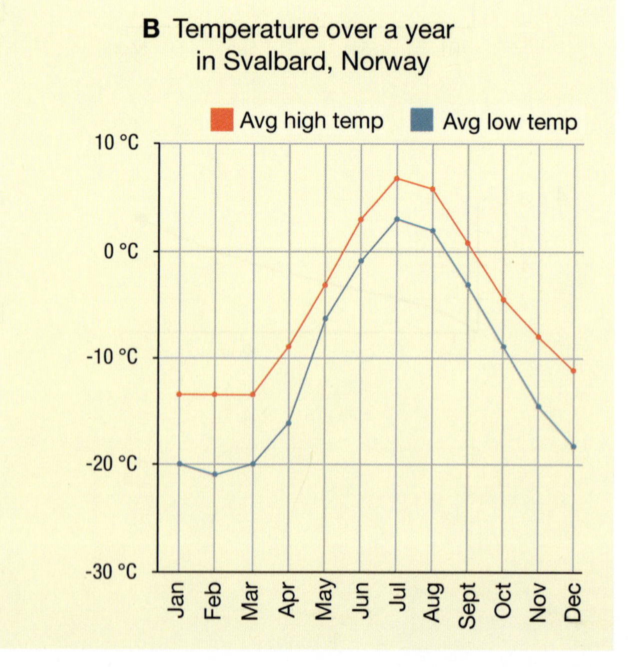

C Precipitation over a year in Amman, Jordan

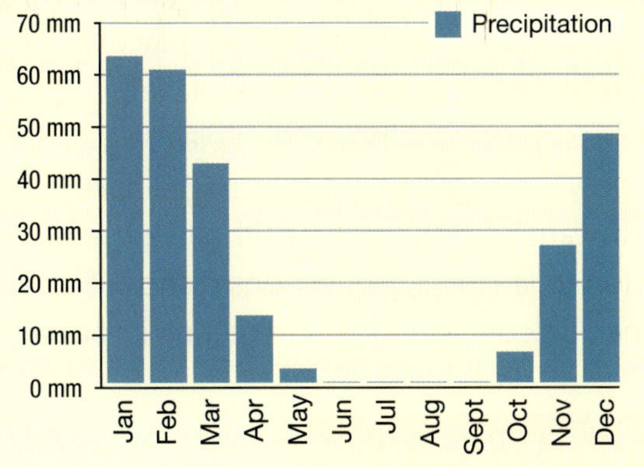

D Temperature over a year in Amman, Jordan

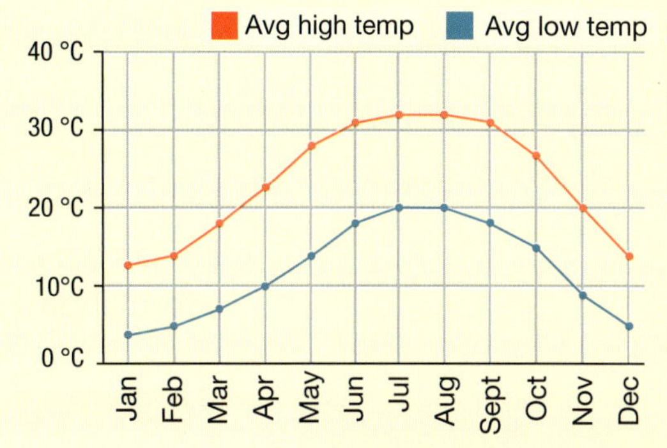

3 Circle the correct words to complete the sentences.

1 Graph A shows *temperature in Celsius / precipitation in millimetres / the number of hurricanes.*
2 Graph B shows *temperature in Celsius / average hours of daylight / precipitation in millimetres.*
3 Graph C shows data for *Amman / Svalbard.*
4 Graph D shows *average temperatures / precipitation.*
5 Graphs A and C are *line graphs / bar charts.*
6 Graphs B and D are *line graphs / bar charts.*

4 Complete the tables, using the information from the graphs in Exercise 2.

Svalbard, Norway

Months	Jan	Feb	Mar	Apr	May	Jun	Jul	Aug	Sept	Oct	Nov	Dec
Precipitation				15 mm			25 mm		25 mm			
Average high temperature	–13 °C				–3 °C						–8 °C	
Average low temperature			–20 °C	–16 °C								–18 °C

Amman, Jordan

Months	Jan	Feb	Mar	Apr	May	Jun	Jul	Aug	Sept	Oct	Nov	Dec
Precipitation		61 mm							0 mm		28 mm	
Average high temperature	13 °C					31 °C						14 °C
Average low temperature			7 °C			18 °C				15 °C		

EVALUATE

5 Look at the graphs and the tables again and answer the questions.

1 Which months have the highest temperatures in each place?
2 Which months have the lowest temperatures in each place?
3 Which months have the most precipitation in each place?
4 Which months have the least precipitation in each place?
5 What extreme weather do you think these places might have?
6 What problems might this cause for the people who live there?
7 Research more information online about questions 6 and 7. Share your information with a partner. Discuss the most interesting information.

GRAMMAR FOR WRITING

COMPARATIVE AND SUPERLATIVE ADJECTIVES

GRAMMAR

Comparative adjectives

Use a comparative adjective + *than* to show how two people, things or ideas are different.

The Sahara Desert is **hotter than** Paris.

For one-syllable adjectives, add *-er*.

warm → **warmer**

For one-syllable adjectives which end in one vowel and one consonant, double the consonant and add *-er*. Do not double the consonant *w*.

wet → **wetter** low → **lower**

NOTE: dry → **drier**

Use *more* before almost all adjectives with two or more syllables. *Less* is the opposite of *more*.

beautiful → **more beautiful / less beautiful**

For two-syllable adjectives ending in *-y*, remove the *-y* and add *-ier*.

rainy → **rainier** early → **earlier**

Some comparative adjectives are irregular.

good → **better** bad → **worse**

Use *as* + adjective + *as* to say that two ideas are similar or the same. *Not as … as* means 'less than'.

Cairo is **as hot as** Dubai. London is **not as hot as** Miami.

GRAMMAR

Superlative adjectives

Use *the* + superlative adjective to compare one person, thing or idea to others. They mean 'more / less than all of the others'.

The Sahara Desert is **the hottest** place in Egypt.

For one-syllable adjectives, add *-est*.

cool → **the coolest** cold → **the coldest**

For one-syllable adjectives which end in one vowel and one consonant, double the consonant and add *-est*. Do not double the consonant *w*.

hot → **the hottest** low → **the lowest**

Use *the most* or *the least* before almost all adjectives with two or more syllables.

dangerous → **the most dangerous** / **the least dangerous**

✗ the ~~most~~ hungriest

For two-syllable adjectives ending in *-y*, remove the *-y* and add *-iest*.

hungry → **the hungriest** early → **the earliest**

Some superlative adjectives are irregular.

good → **the best** bad → **the worst**

1 Complete the table with the correct form of the adjective.

adjective	comparative	superlative
cold		
low		
extreme		
dry		
big		
easy		

2 Choose the comparative or superlative form of the adjectives in Exercise 1 to complete the sentences.

1 This is *drier* / *the driest* year on record. There has been no rain for two months.
2 This winter is *colder* / *the coldest* than last winter. It was –10 °C again yesterday.
3 Our oceans can have some of *more extreme* / *the most extreme* weather on earth.
4 The rainfall was *lower* / *the lowest* this month than last month.
5 In my country, *bigger* / *the biggest* problem is the weather. It's cold and it rains all the time.

3 Look at the fact files for Cuba and Iceland. Complete the sentences, using the word in brackets to make a comparative or superlative adjective.

FACT FILE Cuba

- Maximum temperature: 32 °C
- Minimum temperature: 18 °C
- Average rainfall: 173 mm
- Average sunshine: 7.5 hours a day

FACT FILE Iceland

- Maximum temperature: 14 °C
- Minimum temperature: –2 °C
- Average rainfall: 94 mm
- Average sunshine: 3.4 hours a day

1 Cuba has a ________ maximum temperature than Iceland. (high)
2 Iceland is ________ than Cuba. (cold)
3 Iceland has the ________ temperature of the two countries. (low)
4 Cuba is ________ than Iceland. (wet)
5 Iceland is ________ than Cuba. (dry)
6 Cuba is the ________ of the two countries. (rainy)
7 Iceland is not as ________ as Cuba. (sunny)

ACADEMIC WRITING SKILLS

TOPIC SENTENCES FOR DESCRIPTIVE PARAGRAPHS ABOUT A GRAPH

SKILLS

When writing about a graph, use the phrase *the graph shows* in the topic sentence to describe the information in the graph.

The graph shows the temperature in degrees Celsius over 24 hours in the Sahara desert.

Notice how the following order is used:

The graph shows + what is measured + time period + place.

1 Complete the topic sentences about graphs A and B on page 92 in the Critical thinking section.

1 Graph A shows the ________ in millimetres over one ________ in ________ .

2 Graph B shows the ________ in degrees Celsius over one ________ in ________ .

SUPPORTING SENTENCES

SKILLS

The *supporting sentences* in a paragraph give more information about the topic sentence. When writing about graphs, numbers (or *data*) are used to support main ideas.

Thunderstorms are common all over the world. **Weather experts estimate that there are 16 million thunderstorms around the world every year.**

2 In the pairs of sentences, underline the main idea. Circle the data.

1 The hottest time is between 2 pm and 4 pm. Temperatures rise to 33 °C.
2 The coldest time is at 4 am. Temperatures fall to –1 °C.

3 Match the sentence halves to complete the statements.

1 The main idea — **a** describes a general feature or trend from the graph.
2 The data — **b** is a number from the graph to illustrate the trend.

4 Match the main ideas (1–4) to the data (a–d).

Main ideas

1 New York is as rainy as Houston.
2 The hottest month is March.
3 July is sunnier than August.
4 The coldest month is December.

Data

a There are 8.7 hours of sunshine in July and 8 hours of sunshine in August.
b Temperatures reach 37 °C.
c Both cities have an average rainfall of 1,270 millimetres.
d Temperatures fall to –7 °C.

5 Read the topic sentence. Then tick (✔) all the supporting sentences (a–f) which belong in the paragraph.

Topic sentence: The weather in Costa Rica changes in different regions.

a The rainiest area in the country is the north-east mountain region, which receives 3,580 millimetres of rain each year. ☐
b The Central Valley, where the capital city of San José is located, has the mildest temperature year round. ☐
c In Costa Rica, the rainy season lasts from May to November. ☐
d At the beach, the temperature can rise to as high as 33 °C. ☐
e In the rainforest, there are thousands of different types of animals to see. ☐
f On the highest mountain, called Cerro Chirripó, temperatures can drop to below freezing at night. ☐

GIVING EXAMPLES

SKILLS

like, *such as* and *for example*

In a supporting sentence, writers often give examples to support the main idea. Use *like*, *such as* and *for example* to give an example or a list of examples.

Stay warm by wearing the right clothes, **like** a hat and a sweater.
Hurricanes are usually given names, **such as** Hurricane Sandy.
There are a lot of fun activities to do in the winter, **for example** skiing and ice skating.

Use a comma before *like*, *such as* and *for example*.

6 Rewrite the sentences. Put the words in brackets in the correct place and use *like*, *such as* or *for example*. More than one answer is possible.

1 Wildfires have many different causes. (lightning)
Wildfires have many different causes, like lightning.

2 It is too hot to snow in some Central American cities. (Managua, Guadalajara)

____

3 There are a lot of tornadoes in certain US states. (Oklahoma, Texas)

____

4 When you go camping, bring important items. (water, sunscreen)

____

5 You can do a lot of outdoor activities in warm weather. (swimming, walking)

____

PLUS

6 Some cities are very wet and rainy. (Hong Kong, Mumbai)

____

WRITING TASK

Compare the weather in two places, using information from graphs.

PLAN

1 Look back at the graphs and tables for the places in the Critical thinking section. Write a topic sentence to describe the data in each table.

____

____

____

____

____

2 Choose the two most interesting facts about temperature for each place. Write a sentence about each fact. Use data to support the statements.

____

____

____

____

____

3 Choose the two most interesting facts about precipitation for each place. Write a sentence about each fact. Use data to support the statements.

____

____

____

____

____

4 Refer to the Task checklist on page 100 as you prepare your paragraph.

WRITE A FIRST DRAFT

5 Write a first draft of your paragraph.

REVISE

6 Use the Task checklist to review your paragraph for content and structure.

TASK CHECKLIST	✔
Did you write a topic sentence and supporting sentences?	
Did you give examples with *like*, *such as* and *for example*?	
Did you write about precipitation and temperature?	
Did you compare data from the graphs?	
Have you used data from the graphs to support the main ideas?	

7 Make any necessary changes to your paragraph.

EDIT

8 Use the Language checklist to edit your paragraph for language errors.

LANGUAGE CHECKLIST	✔
Did you use the correct collocations with *temperature*?	
Did you use the correct vocabulary to describe the graphs?	
Did you use comparative and superlative adjectives correctly?	

9 Make any necessary changes to your paragraph.

OBJECTIVES REVIEW

1 Check your learning objectives for this unit. Write *3*, *2* or *1* for each objective.

3 = very well   2 = well   1 = not so well

I can …

watch and understand a video about tornadoes.	____
read for detail.	____
use my knowledge to predict content.	____
analyze graphs.	____
use comparative and superlative adjectives.	____
write topic sentences for descriptive paragraphs about a graph.	____
write supporting sentences.	____
give examples with *like*, *such as* and *for example*.	____
write a paragraph describing data from graphs.	____

2 Use the *Unlock* Digital Workbook for more practice with this unit's learning objectives.

UNLOCK ONLINE

WORDLIST

almost (adv) ⊙	fall (v) ⊙	precipitation (n) ⊙
careful (adj) ⊙	huge (adj) ⊙	reach (v) ⊙
cover (v) ⊙	increase (n, v) ⊙	rise (v) ⊙
dangerous (adj) ⊙	last (v) ⊙	shock (n) ⊙
decide (v) ⊙	lightning (n)	thunder (n)
decrease (n, v) ⊙	maximum (adj) ⊙	
drop (v) ⊙	minimum (adj) ⊙	

⊙ = high-frequency words in the Cambridge Academic Corpus

LEARNING OBJECTIVES	IN THIS UNIT YOU WILL ...
Watch and listen	watch and understand a video about a 96-year-old bungee jumper.
Reading skill	scan to predict content.
Critical thinking	analyze a diagram.
Grammar	use prepositions of movement; use correct subject and verb agreement.
Academic writing skills	order events in a process; remove unrelated information.
Writing task	write a process paragraph.

SPORTS AND COMPETITION

UNIT 5

UNLOCK YOUR KNOWLEDGE

Look at the photo and discuss the questions with a partner.

1 What sport do you see? Do you think it looks fun? Why / Why not?
2 Do you play any sports? Why / Why not?
3 Do you like watching sports? If so, which sports do you enjoy watching?
4 Do you have a favourite team or player?
5 Why do you think people like watching sports?

PLUS

WATCH AND LISTEN

PREPARING TO WATCH

ACTIVATING YOUR KNOWLEDGE

1 Complete the information about bungee jumping with your own ideas. Compare your ideas with a partner.

WHAT DO YOU KNOW ABOUT BUNGEE JUMPING?

1 You jump off a __________ .

2 They tie a rope to your __________ .

3 Bungee jumping is a/an __________ sport.

4 It is not a good idea to bungee jump in __________ weather.

PREDICTING CONTENT USING VISUALS

2 You are going to watch a video about somebody breaking a world record. Before you watch, look at the pictures and answer the questions with your partner.

1 What does the phrase 'world record' mean? Can you think of any famous world records?
2 What world record do you think the man in the pictures broke?
3 How do you think he felt before, during and after breaking the record?

GLOSSARY

injured (adj) When somebody is injured their body is hurt, for example, they break a leg or an arm.

challenge (n) something that is difficult to do

experience (n) something that happens to you that changes how you feel

deafening (adj) very loud

jerk (v) to make a short sudden movement, or to cause someone or something to do this

shake (v) to move quickly from side to side or up and down

WHILE WATCHING

UNDERSTANDING MAIN IDEAS

3 ▶ Watch the video. Circle the correct answers.

1 The world's *oldest* / *first* bungee jumper jumped from the Bloukrans Bridge.
2 Bungee jumping is a *safe* / *dangerous* sport.
3 Mohr Keet bungee jumped *three* / *many* times.
4 It was *rainy* / *windy* when Mohr Keet jumped.
5 Mohr Keet *was* / *was not* injured when he jumped.

UNDERSTANDING DETAIL

4 ▶ Watch again. Complete the answers to the questions.

1 How high is the Bloukrans Bridge?	________ metres.
2 What body parts can be injured in a bungee jump?	The eyes, the ________ and the ________ .
3 How old was Mohr when he did his first jump?	________ years old.
4 How does Mohr feel about being afraid?	He ________ it.
5 Why did Mohr jump?	For the challenge and the ________ .
6 How old was Mohr when he broke the record?	________ years old.

5 ▶ Watch again. Write *T* (true) or *F* (false) next to the statements below. Correct the false statements.

_____ 1 The Bloukrans Bridge is one of the shortest bungee jumps.
_____ 2 Bungee ropes often break.
_____ 3 Mohr's second jump was when he was 93.
_____ 4 Mohr wanted to break a world record.
_____ 5 The wind shook the rope when Mohr jumped.
_____ 6 Mohr thought about his family before he jumped.

DISCUSSION

6 Work with a partner. Discuss the questions.

1 What other sports are dangerous?
2 How do you feel about older people, for example, your grandparents, doing dangerous sports? Why?
3 What are three things you should do before you try a dangerous sport?

READING

READING 1

PREPARING TO READ

UNDERSTANDING KEY VOCABULARY

1 Read the definitions. Complete the sentences with the words in bold.

ancient (adj) from a long time ago; very old
compete (v) to take part in a race or competition; to try to be more successful than someone else
competition (n) an organized event in which people try to win a prize by being the best
strange (adj) not familiar; difficult to understand; different
swimming (n) a sport where people move through water by moving their body
take place (phr v) to happen
throw (v) to send something through the air, pushing it out of your hand

1 The football match will __________ tomorrow at 2 pm in the stadium.
2 Thousands of people from all over the world __________ in the New York City Marathon every year.
3 Boxing is a(n) __________ sport; it was popular in Rome thousands of years ago.
4 The first cricket game I ever saw was __________ because I didn't understand the rules. Once I learnt more about the sport, I became a big fan.
5 In baseball, players must be able to __________ the ball a long distance directly to another player.
6 The best tennis players from each secondary school will play in a(n) __________ to see who is the best player in the city.
7 Because Elsa grew up near the sea, her favourite sport was __________ . She was in the water nearly every day during the summer.

SKILLS

Scanning to predict content

Before reading a text, skilled readers often scan for *key words*. Key words are usually nouns, verbs and adjectives. The key words tell the reader what the text is going to be about. When the reader knows what the text is going to be about, it's easier to understand and easier to read critically.

SCANNING TO PREDICT CONTENT

2 Look at the underlined words in paragraph 1 of the text on page 108. Answer the questions.

1 What is the main topic of the text?
   a unusual competitions
   b unusual sports
   c popular sports
2 Where do the events in the text happen?
   a in one country
   b around the world
   c in a city
3 Look at the underlined words again. What types of words are they? More than one answer is possible.
   a verbs
   b adjectives
   c articles
   d nouns
   e prepositions

3 Read the text and check your answers to Exercise 2.

SPORTING NEWS HOME ABOUT NEWS CONTACT MORE

Five unusual sports

The most unusual sports from around the world

1 Every country has a national sport and most popular sports are now played across the world. Most people have heard of sports like football, basketball, baseball and cricket. However, in most countries, people also play unusual sports with **strange** and interesting rules. Here are our top five unusual sports from around the world.

2 ____________________

People go **swimming** in the Atlantic Ocean in the winter. They go swimming at the beach on Coney Island in New York City every Sunday from October to April and also on New Year's Day. The water temperature can drop to as low as 0 °C. Sometimes there is snow and cold wind, too. People believe that swimming in the cold water is good for their health. The club started in 1903.

3 ____________________

Every year in Singapore, thousands of people come to watch the dragon boat race. A dragon boat is a traditional Chinese boat with a painted dragon's head on one end. There are 22 people in each boat, and they race in the water. Dragon boat racing is also popular in China, Malaysia and Indonesia.

4 ____________________

In this sport, people **compete** by **throwing** a large piece of wood called a 'caber' as far as they can. The caber toss is an **ancient** Scottish sport. The caber has no official size or shape, but it is usually the size of a small tree.

5 ____________________

Students in Indonesia play this game to welcome the month of Ramadan. It is similar to football. The ball is made from coconut shells. Before starting the game, players pour salt on themselves and then set the ball on fire. The ball is on fire throughout the game and the players play with their bare[1] feet.

6 ____________________

In Turkey, camel wrestling[2] is a very old sport. The largest camel wrestling **competition takes place** in Ephesus every year and thousands of people come to watch. In the sport, two male camels wrestle each other. Sometimes the camels do not want to fight and they run through the crowds, which can be dangerous.

[1]**bare** (adj) without shoes

[2]**wrestling** (n) a sport in which two people (or, in this case, animals) fight and try to push each other to the ground

WHILE READING

READING FOR MAIN IDEAS

4 Read the titles below. Write the titles (a–e) above each paragraph (2–6) in the text.

- **a** Fireball football
- **b** Dragon boat racing
- **c** Camel wrestling
- **d** Caber toss
- **e** Coney Island Polar Bear Plunge

5 Write the names of the countries where each sport is popular.

1. Fireball football __________
2. Dragon boat race __________
3. Camel wrestling __________
4. Caber toss __________
5. Coney Island Polar Bear Plunge __________

READING FOR DETAIL

6 Read the text again and look at the sentences. There is one mistake in each sentence. Correct the false information. Then check your answers with a partner.

1. The Coney Island Polar Bear Plunge takes place every Sunday from October to April and on Independence Day.
____
2. The Coney Island Polar Bear Plunge began in 2003.
____
3. A dragon boat has a dragon's tail painted on it.
____
4. There are 25 people in each dragon boat team.
____
5. A caber is a large piece of metal.
____
6. A caber is usually the size of a large tree.
____
7. In fireball football, the ball is made from plastic.
____
8. The ball is on fire only at the beginning of a game of fireball football.
____
9. The Ephesus camel wrestling competition happens twice a year.
____
10. In camel wrestling, two female camels fight each other.
____

READING BETWEEN THE LINES

RECOGNIZING TEXT TYPE

7 Answer the questions.

1 What kind of person is this text for?
   a someone who is interested in different sports
   b someone who wants to learn how to play a new sport
2 Where do you think you might see this text?
   a in a newspaper or magazine
   b on a website
3 What do you think the text is?
   a an advert
   b an article

8 Work with a partner. Check your answers in Exercise 7. Discuss which parts of the text helped you answer the questions.

DISCUSSION

9 Discuss the questions with a partner.

1 Which sport in Reading 1 would you most like to try? Why?
2 Are there any unusual sports in your country? Explain them.

READING 2

PREPARING TO READ

UNDERSTANDING KEY VOCABULARY

1 Read the sentences (1–4) and choose the best definition (a or b) for the words in bold.

1 In January 2018, the Hong Kong Marathon had over 62,000 **participants**.
   a people who take part in an activity
   b people who organize an activity
2 The golf **course** was so big that the players drove golf carts to get from hole to hole.
   a an area used for sporting events, such as racing or playing golf
   b an area where players get together after they finish a sport
3 It takes about six hours to **climb** Mount Fuji in Japan. Many people try to reach the top just before the sun rises.
   a to do something in the shortest time possible
   b to go up or onto the top of something
4 There was an **accident** during the car race yesterday. One car hit another and they both rolled over. Luckily, neither driver was hurt.
   a something bad that happens by mistake and that causes injury or damage
   b something that someone does in order to hurt another person

5 In order to keep **fit**, you should eat foods that are good for you, exercise and stay active.
   a interesting because you like different things
   b in good health; strong
6 One of the most **challenging** games is table tennis, which is also called ping-pong. Players must be strong, quick and able to focus on the ball for long periods of time.
   a easy to learn
   b difficult in a way that tests your ability

PLUS

PREVIEWING

2 Before you read, look at the text on page 112. What type of text is it?

3 Look at the photos and read the title of the text. What do you think the topic of the text will be?

4 Read the text on page 112 and check your answers to Exercises 2 and 3.

WHILE READING

READING FOR MAIN IDEAS

5 Read the text again and circle the correct words to complete the sentences.

1 Tough Guy is a very *easy / difficult* competition.
2 The event takes place when it is very *hot / cold*.
3 People from many different *countries / cities* take part.
4 Every year, people *get hurt / leave early*.
5 Participants have to be very *clever / strong* to do the event.
6 The competition is *different / the same* every year.

READING FOR DETAIL

6 Look at the diagram of the course on page 112. Match the different parts of the competition (1–6) to the facts (a–f) from the final paragraph of the text.

1 mud run
2 nets
3 high dive and swim
4 field of fire
5 water tunnel
6 nettles

a Participants must crawl through something wet.
b The runners run and jump over small bonfires.
c The runners run 2 kilometres through a field of plants that may hurt them.
d Participants run for 1 kilometre along a road that is wet and dirty.
e The runners jump off a platform into a lake and swim for 1 kilometre.
f They crawl low on the ground.

TOUGH[1] GUY:
A race to the limit

1 What is Tough Guy?

Every January, more than 3,000 people take part in one of the most difficult races on Earth: the Tough Guy competition in the UK. **Participants** run, swim and **climb** across the 15-kilometre **course**. But this is no normal race. These runners have to crawl through tunnels, run across a field of nettles and jump over fire. What's more, the competition takes place in January, so temperatures are freezing – sometimes as low as –6 °C. People travel from all over the world to take part, with participants from the US, Australia and China.

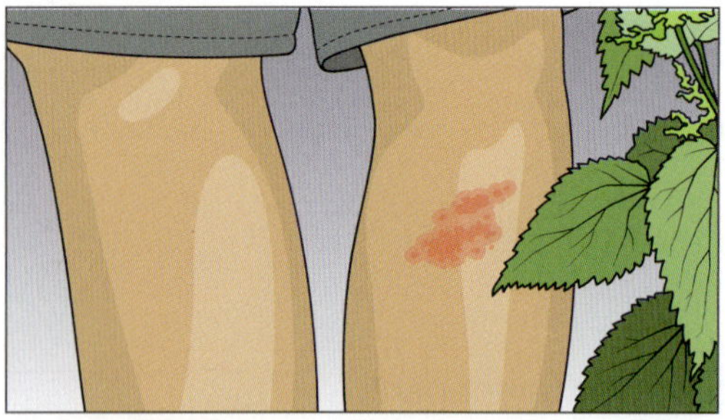

2 Why do people take part?

The competition is very dangerous and every year there are **accidents**. Injuries like broken bones and cuts are common. The race is very hard: one-third of participants do not finish it. Runners have to be **fit** and healthy. Most people train all year to prepare for the event. It is also the first race like it in the world. Many people take part in the competition because it is so famous.

Every year, the organizers change the event and add new things. This means that the competition stays exciting and **challenging**, so people go back year after year.

3 The course

The diagram shows an example of the Tough Guy course. First, participants run for 1 kilometre along a muddy road. Next, they crawl under low nets on the ground. After the nets, the runners jump off a high platform into a lake and swim for another 1 kilometre. Then they reach the field of fire. Here the runners run across a field and jump over small bonfires[2]. Next, participants must crawl through a long tunnel. The tunnel is partly underwater. Finally, the runners run 2 kilometres through nettles before they reach the finish line.

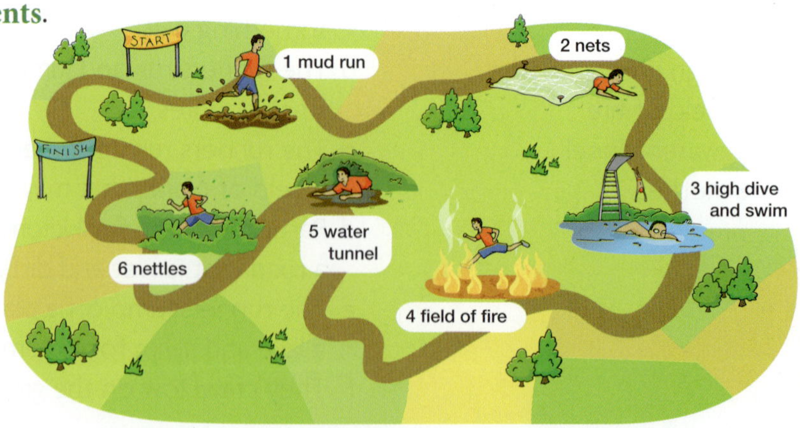

[1]**tough** (adj) physically strong and not afraid
[2]**bonfires** (n) outdoor fires that burn waste

7 Answer the questions.

1 Where does the Tough Guy competition take place?

____

2 When does the Tough Guy competition take place?

____

3 How long is the course? ______________________

4 How long do people train for the competition? ______________________

5 Why do people go back to the competition every year?

____

UNDERSTANDING DISCOURSE

8 Match the verbs (1–3) to the correct phrases (a–f). Each verb has two answers.

1 crawl	a over small bonfires
2 run	b across a field of nettles
3 jump	c under low nets
	d across a field of fire
	e through tunnels
	f off a high platform

READING BETWEEN THE LINES

WORKING OUT MEANING FROM CONTEXT

9 Circle the correct answer.

1 The text says that participants have to *run through nettles*. Look at the images and the text. What is a nettle?
   a a plant
   b an animal

2 Why do you think running through nettles is difficult?
   a because nettles hurt you
   b because nettles smell horrible

DISCUSSION

SYNTHESIZING

10 Use ideas from Reading 1 and Reading 2 to answer the following questions with a partner.

1 Would you do the Tough Guy competition? Why / Why not? Would any of your friends or family do it?

2 Should people be allowed to participate in dangerous sports? How can people protect themselves when playing these sports?

PLUS

LANGUAGE DEVELOPMENT

PREPOSITIONS OF MOVEMENT

GRAMMAR

Prepositions of movement describe where someone or something is going. Use prepositions of movement to give directions.

Walk **past** the school and **across** the road.

1 Match the descriptions (1–7) to the pictures (a–g).

1 past the building
2 through the tunnel
3 across the lake
4 around the track
5 along the road
6 over the bridge
7 under the bridge

a

b

c

d

e

f

g

2 Look at the map. Use the prepositions from Exercise 1 to complete the paragraph. You may need to use some prepositions more than once.

PLUS

It is easy to get to my house. First, walk (1)__________ the High Street. Go (2)__________ the bank and (3)__________ the bridge. Then walk (4)__________ the park and (5)__________ the next bridge. Go (6)__________ the tunnel – watch out for cars – and walk (7)__________ the road. Walk (8)__________ the lake. My house is at the end of the road. It's the pink one!

WRITING

CRITICAL THINKING

At the end of this unit, you will write a process paragraph. Look at this unit's writing task below.

Describe the Sydney Triathlon.

SKILLS

Analyzing a diagram

Diagrams are useful because they show information in a clear and interesting way. Before writing about a diagram, it is important to understand what the different parts of the diagram are showing, for example the order of events and the effect that different events have on each other.

ANALYZE

1 A triathlon is a race in which people swim, cycle and run without stopping between events. Look at the diagram of the triathlon course in Sydney, Australia. Label the diagram with the words from the box. Use the key to help you.

bridge	central library	cycle route
running route	tunnel	swimming route

2 Look at the diagram again and answer the questions.

1 How far do the participants have to run?

____

2 How far do the participants have to swim?

____

3 How far do the participants have to cycle?

____

3 Look at the diagram again. What do the competitors in the triathlon have to do? Use prepositions to complete the phrases.

a cycle _________ the bridge
b cycle _________ the tunnel
c run _________ the road
d swim _________ the bay
e cycle _________ the central library

4 Number the parts of the race (a–e) in Exercise 3 to show the correct order of the triathlon (1–5).

GRAMMAR FOR WRITING

SUBJECT AND VERB AGREEMENT

GRAMMAR

In a sentence, the form of the verb has to match the subject.

Use the *singular* form of the verb with singular subjects.
The race **begins** at 3 pm.
The winner of last year's race **is** at the starting line.

Use the *plural* form of the verb with plural subjects.
The footballers **play** three times a week.
Football and tennis **are** popular sports.

1 Look at the sentences. Underline the subject and circle the verb.

1 The boys and girls play sports every day.
2 We watch the World Cup finals at home.
3 Aisha runs across the field.
4 Football is a popular sport in Europe.
5 You run over the bridge.
6 Hanh and I love motor racing.

2 Circle the correct form of the verb in the sentences.

1 Julia *is* / *are* a tennis player.
2 The coach *swim* / *swims* every day.
3 Jenny and I *cycle* / *cycles* to work every day.
4 The fastest runner *win* / *wins* the trophy.
5 Oleg and I *practise* / *practises* hockey after school.
6 Skiing *are* / *is* a winter sport.

3 Complete the sentences with the correct form of the verb in brackets. Use the present simple tense only.

1 I ________ (try) to practise every day.
2 The team captain ________ (carry) the trophy.
3 Dragon boat racing ________ (be) an unusual sport.
4 My friends and I ________ (watch) sports on TV.
5 Footballers often ________ (miss) penalties.
6 He ________ (want) to be a Formula One driver.
7 The teams and the referee ________ (run) onto the field.
8 Cricket and rugby ________ (be) popular sports in the UK.
9 The players ________ (catch) the ball.

ACADEMIC WRITING SKILLS

ORDERING EVENTS IN A PROCESS

SKILLS

When writing about a process, academic writers usually write about events in the order that they happen. *Transition words* are used to organize ideas and show the order in writing.

Use the transition words *first*, *next*, *then*, *after that* and *finally* to show the order in which events happen in a process.

First, the participants run ten kilometres. **Next**, they swim across the river.
Participants run ten kilometres. **Then**, they swim across the river.

Use these transition words at the beginning of a sentence, followed by a comma.

1 Match the sentences (1–4) to the pictures (a–d).

1 The weightlifter lifts the weight onto his shoulders. ______
2 The weightlifter drops the weight to the ground. ______
3 The weightlifter lifts the weight above his head. ______
4 The weightlifter holds the weight above his head for as long as he can. ______

a

b

c

d

2 Rewrite the sentences in Exercise 1 in the correct order using *first*, *next*, *then*, *after that* and *finally*.

1 ______________________________

____

2 ______________________________

____

3 ______________________________

____

4 ______________________________

____

3 Rewrite the paragraph with the words from the box to show the order of the events. Remember to use commas. More than one answer is possible.

after that	next	then

First, the tennis players walk onto the court. They pick up their rackets. One player hits the ball over the net. The other player hits the ball back.

____

____

____

____

4 Compare and discuss your answers with a partner.

REMOVING UNRELATED INFORMATION

SKILLS

When writing, it is important to write only about information that is related to or useful for the topic. Before you write, decide what information is important and only write about information that is directly related to or useful for the question. After you finish, it is a good idea to check for any information that is not important and delete it.

5 Read the writing task and the student's paragraph. Cross out the information in the paragraph that is not important. Analyze the task carefully to decide what is important.

Write a process paragraph to describe how to do the high jump.

The high jump is an Olympic sport that is practised in many countries. ~~Athletes competed in over 30 venues during the 2012 London Olympic Games~~. First, the high jumper runs towards the bar. It is important to run very fast. The high jump is the most popular sport in Russia. Next, the high jumper jumps. I was on the track-and-field team at school. The high jumper must jump from the right foot and keep their arms close to their sides. Then, the high jumper twists their body so that their back is to the bar. They must lift their head and feet and keep them high above the bar. The high jump is a really interesting sport. After that, the high jumper lands. They must be careful to land safely on the mat. Derek Drouin from Canada won the gold medal in the men's high jump at the 2016 Rio Olympic Games, and Ruth Beitia from Spain won the gold for the women's high jump. Finally, the high jumper stands up, takes a bow and leaves the mat.

6 Compare and discuss your answers with a partner.

WRITING TASK

Describe the Sydney Triathlon.

PLAN

1 Use your notes from the Critical thinking section to complete the paragraph planner. Write any general information that you think might be useful in column A. Put the events in the Sydney Triathlon in the correct order in column B.

A	B
	1
	2
	3
	4
	5

2 Refer to the Task checklist on page 122 as you prepare your paragraph.

WRITE A FIRST DRAFT

3 Start your paragraph by writing a topic sentence about the general information in the diagram.

4 Write supporting sentences about the events in the triathlon in the correct order and use transition words to show the time order.

REVISE

5 Use the Task checklist to review your paragraph for content and structure.

TASK CHECKLIST	✔
Did you write about the general information and the events in the Sydney Triathlon?	
Did you put the events in the correct order?	
Did you use transition words to show the order of the events clearly?	
Did you avoid using unrelated information?	

6 Make any necessary changes to your paragraph.

EDIT

7 Use the Language checklist to edit your paragraph for language errors.

LANGUAGE CHECKLIST	✔
Did you use the correct prepositions of movement?	
Did you use subject and verb agreement correctly?	

8 Make any necessary changes to your paragraph.

OBJECTIVES REVIEW

1 Check your learning objectives for this unit. Write *3*, *2* or *1* for each objective.

3 = very well 2 = well 1 = not so well

I can …

watch and understand a video about a 96-year-old bungee jumper.	_____
scan to predict content.	_____
analyze a diagram.	_____
use prepositions of movement.	_____
use correct subject and verb agreement.	_____
order events in a process.	_____
remove unrelated information.	_____
write a process paragraph.	_____

2 Use the *Unlock* Digital Workbook for more practice with this unit's learning objectives.

UNLOCK ONLINE

WORDLIST

accident (n) ⊙	competition (n) ⊙	swimming (n)
ancient (adj) ⊙	course (n) ⊙	take place (phr v)
challenging (adj) ⊙	fit (adj) ⊙	throw (v) ⊙
climb (v)	participant (n) ⊙	
compete (v) ⊙	strange (adj) ⊙	

⊙ = high-frequency words in the Cambridge Academic Corpus

LEARNING OBJECTIVES	IN THIS UNIT YOU WILL ...
Watch and listen	watch and understand a video about Amazon's fulfilment centre.
Reading skills	work out meaning from context; annotate a text.
Critical thinking	organize events in time order.
Grammar	use the present simple and the past simple; use time clauses with *when* to describe past events.
Academic writing skill	add details to main facts.
Writing task	write a narrative paragraph.

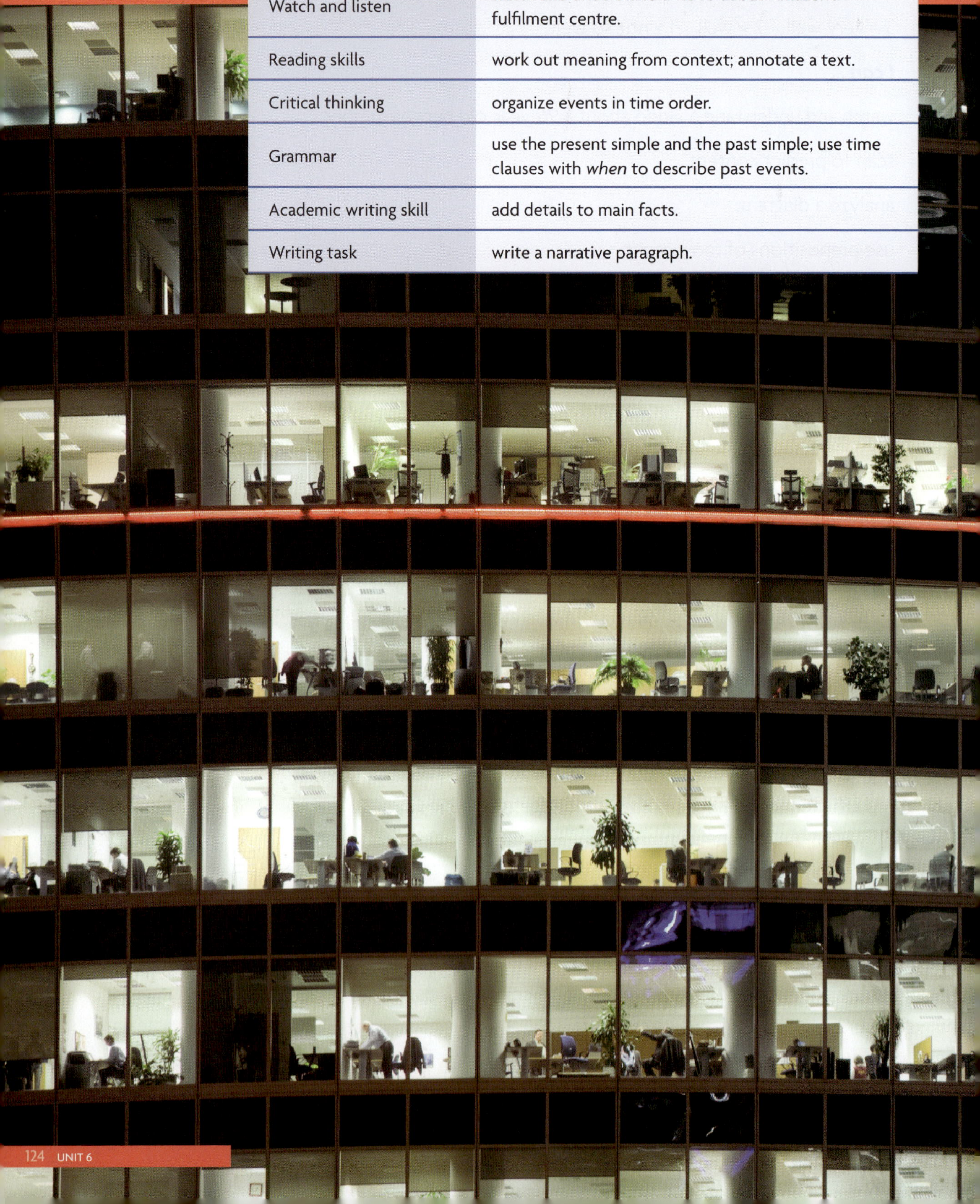

BUSINESS

UNIT 6

UNLOCK YOUR KNOWLEDGE

1 Discuss the questions with a partner.
   a An *entrepreneur* is a person who starts a new business. Do you know the names of the famous entrepreneurs in the photos?
   b Do you know what they are famous for?
   c Do you know the names of any famous entrepreneurs from your country?

2 Look at the words in the box. Which of the words can you use to talk about a successful entrepreneur?

careful	clever	friendly	funny
good with computers	good with money		
happy	hard-working	kind	polite

3 Do you think you would be a good entrepreneur? Why / Why not?

PLUS

WATCH AND LISTEN

PREPARING TO WATCH

ACTIVATING YOUR KNOWLEDGE

1 Work with a partner and answer the questions.

1 Why do people shop online?
2 What do people usually buy online?
3 What was the last thing you bought online? What about in a shop?

USING YOUR KNOWLEDGE

2 You are going to watch a video about the online shop Amazon. Read the statements. Tick (✔) the ones that you think are true.

1 ☐ There are millions of things to buy at Amazon.
2 ☐ A computer finds your things after you order them.
3 ☐ Amazon does not sell kitchen items.

GLOSSARY

warehouse (n) a large building for keeping things that are going to be sold
item (n) a single thing in a set or on a list, such as a book or a toy
fulfilment (n) the act of doing something that you promised to do
central (adj) main or most important; organized and working from one main place
random (adj) done or chosen without any plan or system

WHILE WATCHING

3 Watch the video. Check your answers in Exercise 2.

UNDERSTANDING DETAIL

4 Watch again. Put a tick (✔) next to the things you see.

1 ☐	a shelf	6 ☐	a male worker
2 ☐	a yellow bin	7 ☐	a toy
3 ☐	a warehouse	8 ☐	a computer
4 ☐	a book	9 ☐	a box
5 ☐	a large trolley	10 ☐	tape

5 ▶ Watch again. Complete the summary with numbers or words. Check your answers with a partner.

SUMMARIZING

Amazon's first warehouse was in (1)__________, Washington, in the US. It has more than (2)__________ million items for sale on its (3)__________. Amazon has many (4)__________ warehouses around the world. They are called (5)__________ centres.

6 Write *T* (true) or *F* (false) next to the statements. Correct the false statements.

UNDERSTANDING MAIN IDEAS

_____ 1 Amazon is the world's largest online shop.
_____ 2 The first warehouse was a kitchen.
_____ 3 Only the workers know where everything is.
_____ 4 An Amazon worker finds your item before you pay for it.
_____ 5 Any item can be on any shelf in the warehouse.

7 Put the sentences (a–e) in the order that they happen in the video (1–5). Compare your answers with a partner.

a The box leaves the warehouse. _____
b The computer tells the workers the correct size of the box. _____
c An Amazon worker finds your item. _____
d You order and pay for an item online. _____
e Your name and address go on the box. _____

8 Work with a partner. Why does the speaker in the video say that 'an item's location is random so that workers don't take the wrong item'? Circle the best answer.

MAKING INFERENCES

a The central computer always makes mistakes.
b The worker might choose the wrong item if two similar items were together.
c Amazon trusts its computers more than its workers.

DISCUSSION

9 Work with a partner. Discuss the questions. Explain your answers.

1 In the future, what jobs will computers do that people do today?
2 What jobs will humans always do?
3 What do you think is the future of physical shops?
4 Which items in the box are better to buy in a shop than online?

books	clothes	glasses	food	furniture
jewellery	music	plants	tickets	vitamins

READING

READING 1

PREPARING TO READ

UNDERSTANDING KEY VOCABULARY

1 Read the sentences (1–6) and choose the best definition (a or b) for the words in bold.

1 Marta likes to **organize** her schedule at work. She puts her meetings and tasks in a calendar so that she gets everything done on time.
   a plan or arrange carefully
   b display something for others to see
2 Ken found a job he wants to do. He wants to **apply** for it this week and hopes to get the job.
   a share thoughts and ideas
   b ask officially for something, often by writing
3 Emre just shared the **results** of the company survey. They show that a lot of people are happy with the company's work.
   a information that you find out from something, such as an exam, a scientific experiment or a medical test
   b a list of questions that several people are asked so that information can be collected about something
4 Grace is trying to decide on an **occupation**. She studied business, so there are lots of things she can do.
   a a course of study   b a job or career
5 My **colleague** and I are writing a new computer program. We work late every night because our boss wants us to finish it quickly.
   a someone you live next to   b someone you work with
6 The new shop on the High Street is doing really well. A lot of **customers** go there and buy things.
   a people who buy things from a shop or business
   b people who sell things at a shop or business

SKIMMING

2 Before you read, look at the text on page 129 quickly. Circle the answers.

1 What kind of text is it?
   a a dictionary entry
   b an online quiz
   c a textbook
2 Which question is the best description of the topic?
   a What would be your perfect job?
   b Could you start your own company?
   c What makes a good businessperson?

3 Read the text and check your answers.

Home About Us News Quiz Contact Us More

ARE YOU READY FOR THE WORLD OF WORK?

Do you know what kind of job you want? Before you **apply** for a job, think about the different types of jobs that people do. There are four main types of jobs:

1 jobs with people
2 jobs with information
3 jobs with things
4 jobs with ideas

What kind of work would be best for you? Take our quiz and find out about the kind of work you would enjoy. For each question, choose the best answer for you: a, b, c or d.

Check your **results** and read the advice to find **occupations** you would like.

1 What do you like to do in the evenings?
- ☐ a meet friends or go to a party
- ☐ b stay at home and surf the internet
- ☐ c play sports or practise a hobby like a musical instrument or photography
- ☐ d go to the cinema

2 Which sections of the newspaper do you look at first?
- ☐ a advice column or letters to the editor
- ☐ b news
- ☐ c sport
- ☐ d TV, music, books and art

3 What do you like to do at a party?
- ☐ a meet new people
- ☐ b discuss the latest news
- ☐ c help with the food and drinks
- ☐ d sing songs and tell jokes

4 What do you prefer to do on a day off?
- ☐ a have coffee with friends
- ☐ b **organize** your books and cupboards
- ☐ c work in the garden or clean the house
- ☐ d write poetry, make music or draw pictures

Mostly 'a' answers:
You are friendly, kind and interested in other people. You would enjoy a job working with children, **customers** in a shop or on a team with **colleagues**. Possible jobs are: teacher, waiter, police officer.

Mostly 'b' answers:
You are neat, good at planning and you like learning new things. You would enjoy a job working with information. Possible jobs are: university professor, computer programmer, librarian.

Mostly 'c' answers:
You are practical, good at sports and you like working with your hands. You would enjoy a job working with things. Possible jobs are: construction worker, engineer, farmer.

Mostly 'd' answers:
You are creative, good at music and art and you like books. You would enjoy a job working with ideas. Possible jobs are: artist, writer, singer.

WHILE READING

READING FOR MAIN IDEAS

4 Read the quiz again. Correct the mistakes in the paragraph, using words from the quiz.

> There are three main kinds of jobs – jobs with animals, jobs with information, jobs with machines and jobs with ideas. The quiz helps you to find out about the kind of people you might like. After doing the quiz, read the advice to find universities you might like.

READING FOR DETAIL

5 Do the quiz in the text. Circle your answers and count the letters you chose. Read the advice about jobs for you.

6 Do you agree or disagree with the advice? Why?

READING BETWEEN THE LINES

SKILLS

Working out meaning from context

Readers often see words in a text that they do not know. However, it is often possible to understand the meaning of new words in a text from the context (the topic and the other words in the text).

WORKING OUT MEANING FROM CONTEXT

7 Find the words from the box in the quiz and underline them.

advice	hobby	neat	sections

8 Read the text around the underlined words in the quiz. Circle the best definition (a or b) for each word.

1 advice (n)
  - **a** instructions to tell someone exactly how to do something
  - **b** an opinion that someone offers you about what you should do

2 hobby (n)
  - **a** an activity you do for fun
  - **b** a job you do for no money

3 neat (adj)
  - **a** arranged well, with everything in its place
  - **b** not arranged well, without order

4 section (n)
  - **a** a type of reading material in which you answer questions
  - **b** one of the parts that something is divided into

9 Who would be interested in the quiz? Why? Circle the correct answer. More than one answer is possible.

a a new worker in a company
b a new university graduate
c a secondary school student

IDENTIFYING AUDIENCE

DISCUSSION

10 Discuss the questions with a partner.

1 What would be your perfect job?
2 What type of job would you hate?

READING 2

PREPARING TO READ

UNDERSTANDING KEY VOCABULARY

1 Read the sentences (1–8) and write the correct form of the words in bold next to the definitions (a–h).

1 I want to be a doctor. I can reach my **goal** by studying hard.
2 The company **introduced** a new tablet and it sold out in one day.
3 A lot of new jobs were created by the car factory. They **employ** more than 300 people in the community.
4 I share an **office** with Akiko. It is small and we don't have a lot of space for our desks and files.
5 Manuel is my business **partner**. We opened a restaurant together.
6 I'm going to **set up** a new business selling gifts online.
7 The company needs to **advertise** its new smartphone on TV and on the internet, so that more people know about it and want to buy it.
8 My mother **runs** her own business.

a ________ (phr v) to create or establish (something) for a particular purpose
b ________ (n) a place in a building where people work
c ________ (v) to manage or operate something
d ________ (n) someone who runs or owns a business with another person
e ________ (n) something you want to do successfully in the future
f ________ (v) to pay someone to work or do a job for you
g ________ (v) to make something available to buy or use for the first time
h ________ (v) to tell people about a product or service, for example, in newspapers or on television, in order to persuade them to buy it

PLUS

SCANNING TO PREDICT CONTENT

2 Look at the article on page 133 and notice the words in bold from Exercise 1. Read the title. What do you think the article is about?

WHILE READING

SKILLS

Annotating a text

Effective readers take notes and *annotate* as they read. When you annotate, you write notes on the same page as the text. Annotating will help you to remember key information. For example, you can underline, circle or highlight important words, numbers and ideas. You can write main ideas and definitions of words in the margin. Annotating a text can also help you to study for tests or write about a text. For example:

> all the people able to work
>
> A recent study showed that 10% of the American workforce is made up of self-employed workers. The self-employed then provide jobs for an additional 29 million people.

3 As you read the text, annotate the important words, dates, numbers and ideas.

READING FOR MAIN IDEAS

4 Look at the headings (a–c). Which paragraph (1–3) in the text does each one describe?

a Ideas and creativity Paragraph ______
b Goals then and now Paragraph ______
c The growth of Google Paragraph ______

5 Read the questions (1–4) and circle the correct answers (a–b).

1 How does Google help new businesses?
  a Google lets new businesses borrow money.
  b Google helps new businesses find customers.
2 Where was Google's first office?
  a in a garage
  b at Stanford University
3 What does Google want its employees to do?
  a share creative ideas with each other
  b work at night and sometimes on weekends
4 Who might benefit from a self-driving car?
  a people who have trouble seeing
  b people who drive long distances to work

THE STORY OF GOOGLE

1 Google is a huge technology company. It specializes in online advertising and searching, as well as other internet-related products. Google was started by Larry Page and Sergey Brin. They met at Stanford University in the US in 1995. Their **goal** was to organize all of the information on the web. Today, their company **employs** more than 40,000 people around the world. The two **partners** created a company that made searching the internet easy. Now they focus on three main areas. They make sure their search engine[1] is fast and smart so that people can find information easily. They develop products that let people work on different devices and in different places. They help new businesses **advertise** and find new customers.

2 Google grew very quickly. Page and Brin registered[2] the domain name[3] Google.com in 1997. In 1998, they **set up** a small **office** in a garage and hired their first employee, Craig Silverstein. They **ran** their business in the garage until they could move to a larger space. In the busy years that followed, Google expanded its services. In 2000, people could do internet searches in 15 languages, including Dutch, Chinese and Korean. Today, people can search in about 150 languages. Google **introduced** a map service in 2005 called Google Maps™. The same year, it came out with a program called Google Earth™. This program allowed users to see close-up pictures of cities and neighbourhoods when they typed in an address. In 2006, the name 'Google' became a verb in English dictionaries. This shows the company's influence on modern life.

Larry Page and Sergey Brin

3 Today, Google is a creative workplace where employees share ideas with each other. Page and Brin are available during the week to talk with their employees and answer questions. This open environment has resulted in many new ideas. In 2011, the company released a program called Google Art Project™ which helped people to explore the world's top museums from their computer. As of 2017, Google was continuing its work on a self-driving car. In the future, this car could help people who can't see well to drive. The company extends its services to the community, too. In 2008, it started a yearly art contest for students. Every year, the winner's artwork appears on its home page for one day. Google believes that creativity is important, both in the workplace and in the community. In addition to producing famous internet products, Google gives people opportunities to be creative, which leads to success.

[1]**search engine** (n) a website used for finding specific information on the internet
[2]**registered** (v) put information on an official list
[3]**domain name** (n) the part of an email address or website address that shows the name of the organization that the address belongs to

READING FOR DETAIL

6 Write *T* (true) or *F* (false) next to the statements. Then correct the false statements.

_____ 1 Google's only focus is on making their search engine smart and fast.

____

_____ 2 In 2006, 'Google' was added to dictionaries as a verb.

____

_____ 3 The original Google partners answer questions their employees may have.

____

_____ 4 Google released a program which teaches people how to draw famous works of art.

____

7 Look at the events from the Google business story in the table.

1 In column A, write the year of each event.
2 In column B, number the events in the order that they happened.

	A year	B event
a Google searches could be done in 15 languages.		
b Google started an art contest for students.		
c The partners registered the domain name Google.com.		
d Google introduced a map service.		

READING BETWEEN THE LINES

MAKING INFERENCES

8 Which of the statements is closest to what the creators of Google think? Circle the correct answer.

a It is necessary to be creative if you want to be successful.
b Creativity is not important.
c Creativity can be helpful, but it is not essential.

9 In which paragraph did you find the answer? _____

DISCUSSION

SYNTHESIZING

10 Work with a partner. Use ideas from Reading 1 and Reading 2 to answer the questions.

1 Look again at the quiz in Reading 1. What type of person would fit into the culture of Google? What kinds of skills do you think you need to work for Google?
2 Would you like to work at a large company like Google? Why / Why not?

PLUS

LANGUAGE DEVELOPMENT

COLLOCATIONS WITH *BUSINESS*

a *a plan* ___

f *set up* ___ **b** *a partner* ___

business

e *run* ___ **c** *expand* ___

d *a contact* ___

1 The words in the diagram are collocations of *business*. Write *N* next to the nouns and *V* next to the verbs.

2 Use words (a–f) from the diagram to complete the sentences (1–6).

1 **A business** __________ is a detailed document describing the future direction of a business.
2 __________ **a business** means to make a business bigger.
3 **A business** __________ is a person who owns a business with you.
4 __________ **a business** means to be in charge of and control a business.
5 __________ **a business** means to start a business.
6 **A business** __________ is a person you know because of your job.

PLUS

3 Look at the sentences in Exercise 2 again and answer the questions.

1 Do the verbs go before or after the word *business*? __________
2 Do the nouns go before or after the word *business*? __________

BUSINESS VOCABULARY

4 Match the words (1–8) to their definitions (a–h).

1 colleague	**a** a program you use to control what a computer does
2 department	**b** something a business makes and sells
3 employ	**c** someone that you work with
4 employee	**d** a place in a building where people work
5 manager	**e** the person who organizes or leads a business
6 office	**f** to pay someone to work or do a job for you
7 product	**g** part of a business or company
8 software	**h** a worker

5 Use the words from Exercise 4 to complete the email. You may need to use the plural form of some words.

To: Sales and marketing department
From: Jane Curry
Subject: Important information

Important information for (1)__________ of Jenson Co.

I am pleased to tell you that we are moving into a bright new (2)__________ in three months. We are also getting new (3)__________ for our computers. We will have more space, so we can (4)__________ more people.

I am very confident that these changes will help us sell more of our excellent (5)__________ . It is exciting that our (6)__________ continues to grow. You and your (7)__________ are responsible for that.

Best,

Jane Curry

General (8)__________

PLUS

WRITING

CRITICAL THINKING

At the end of this unit, you will write a narrative paragraph. Look at this unit's writing task below.

Write a narrative paragraph about the history of a business.

EVALUATE

1 Look back at Reading 2 on page 133. Which years in the text were particularly important for Google? Choose 2–3 important events.

1 ______________________________

2 ______________________________

3 ______________________________

2 Discuss the years you chose with a partner.

SKILLS

Organizing events in time order

When writing about things that happened in the past, writers often put them in time order. First, you should select the key events. Then, you should identify the first event that happened and end with the event that happened last. Timelines are a useful way to organize past events in time order.

APPLY

3 Use the notes and annotations you made in Reading 2 to place the events in Google's history below in the correct place on the timeline. Write the dates above the timeline and the events below it.

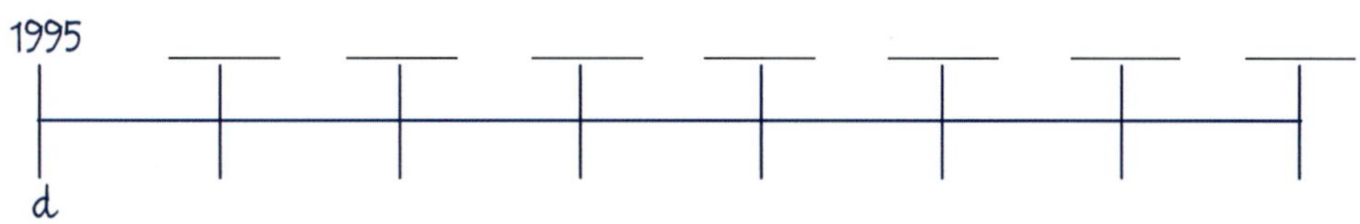

a Google Earth™ and Google Maps™ are launched.

b Google employs its first worker, Craig Silverstein.

c Page and Brin register the domain name Google.com.

~~**d** Larry Page and Sergey Brin meet at Stanford University.~~

e Google starts its student art contest.

f 'Google' becomes a verb in English dictionaries.

g It becomes possible to search Google in 15 languages.

h Google Art Project™ is launched.

CREATE

4 Look up information about a business you are interested in. Find information about the business on the internet. Choose a business that is well-known so there will be a lot of information available. Identify eight key dates in the history of the business. Write the dates on the timeline below.

5 Write the events in time order next to the letters a–h, as in Exercise 3. Do not use more than eight words to describe each event.

a ______________________________

b ______________________________

c ______________________________

d ______________________________

e ______________________________

f ______________________________

g ______________________________

h ______________________________

6 Add any other interesting information that you found about the business in the box below. You can also add details to the events you describe in Exercise 5 in the relevant section.

General notes:	
a	
b	
c	
d	
e	
f	
g	
h	

GRAMMAR FOR WRITING

THE PRESENT SIMPLE AND THE PAST SIMPLE

GRAMMAR

Use the *present simple* to talk about things which happen regularly, or which are true in general.

Employees **share** ideas with each other.

The company **employs** more than 40,000 people around the world.

Use the *past simple* to talk about events that happened in the past.

The two partners **created** a company that **made** searching the internet easy.

1 Circle the verbs in the sentences. Write *past* next to the verbs in the past simple and *present* next to the verbs in the present simple.

1 Ford is one of the most famous motor companies in the world.
2 Jacques Nasser joined Ford in 1968.
3 Jacques Nasser is the son of Abdo Nasser.
4 On 1 January 1999, Jacques Nasser became president of Ford.
5 In 2000, Ford bought Land Rover.
6 In 2003, Ford celebrated its 100th birthday.

2 Circle the correct form of the verbs in the paragraph.

The JLX company (1) *sells / sold* food to supermarkets and shops. In 2009, Martha Underwood (2) *sets up / set up* the business. In 2010, the company (3) *does / did* very well. In June, Martha Underwood (4) *employs / employed* three new employees. The company (5) *expands / expanded* and (6) *opens / opened* new offices in Europe. Today, JLX (7) *is / was* a very successful business.

3 Write the correct form of the verbs in brackets. Use the past simple or present simple.

1 Nissan ____________ (be) a Japanese company.
2 In 1824, John Cadbury ____________ (open) the first Cadbury's chocolate shop.
3 Lego ____________ (sell) toys.
4 Today, Nestlé ____________ (be) the world's biggest food and drinks business.
5 Nokia ____________ (start) in 1865.
6 In 1995, Amazon ____________ (sell) the first book on Amazon.com.
7 Adidas ____________ (make) sports clothes around the world.
8 In 1926, Mercedes-Benz ____________ (design) its first car.

4 Complete the sentences with the past simple form of the words in the box.

be	become	begin	graduate	vote

1 In 2016, Alibaba ____________ one of the largest internet companies in the world.
2 Indra Nooyi was born in India, ____________ from Yale University and is the CEO of PepsiCo.
3 Peugeot is a French car company. It ____________ as a family business in 1810.
4 In 2017, passengers ____________ Qatar Airways the best airline in the world.
5 Before she wrote books, J. K. Rowling ____________ a teacher.

TIME CLAUSES WITH *WHEN* TO DESCRIBE PAST EVENTS

GRAMMAR

Use a time clause with *when* to describe the date or time that something happened in the past.

time clause: when he was sixteen

He started the business **when** he was sixteen.

To make the time of the event more important, put the time clause with *when* first and follow it with a comma.

time clause: When he was sixteen

When he was sixteen, he started the business.

5 Rewrite the sentences using time clauses with *when*.

1 She became the CEO. She was 30.

____

2 They employed six new workers. The business expanded.

____

3 He left his job. He was 65.

____

4 The shop closed. The economy crashed.

____

5 They expanded the company. It was still successful.

____

6 Put the words in order to make complete sentences.

1 a company / When Lei / her master's degree, / she started / finished / .

____

2 when / was one year old / The owners opened / the first one / a second café / .

____

3 he advertised / online / When Samir / to get more customers, / wanted / his business / .

____

4 Anika loved / she was / computers when / a child / about / to learn / .

____

5 When / a bigger office / she moved / CEO / became / Yoko / to / .

____

ACADEMIC WRITING SKILLS

ADDING DETAILS TO MAIN FACTS

SKILLS

In a narrative paragraph, adding details to the main facts makes the writing more interesting and informative. Giving examples and reasons, explaining ideas and using adjectives are ways to add details.

The details should help your readers form a picture of the events in their minds. Ask yourself these questions to help add detail to narrative writing:

- Who or what is the paragraph about?
- Why did the events happen?
- How can I help the reader make a mental picture of what I am describing?
- Can I make any information more specific with dates, reasons, adjectives or examples?
- Do the details in my narrative tell the story?

1 Read about the history of YouTube. The sentences below the text add more detail. Write the letters of the sentences in the correct places in the paragraph.

> In 2005, three friends, Chad Hurley, Steve Chen and Jawed Karim, had an idea for an internet business. (1)_____ They created YouTube™. Today, YouTube is the largest video sharing site on the internet, and it has over 1.5 billion users. YouTube's first office was located in a simple room. (2)_____ Their first video was posted in April 2005. It was called 'Me at the Zoo'. (3)_____ Within five months, over a million people saw the video. Businesses began to notice YouTube and wanted to advertise on the website. In July 2006, 65,000 new videos were posted every day. In November 2006, Google bought YouTube. (4)_____

a They wanted to help people share videos on the internet.
b It showed Karim at the zoo talking about elephants.
c They paid the incredible price of $1.65 billion.
d The room was located above a pizza restaurant in Menlo Park, California, in the US.

PLUS

2 Look back at the completed timeline in Exercise 3 of the Critical thinking section. Write the letter of the main facts in the Google story timeline next to the matching details below.

1 Google Earth™ is a map that shows close-up pictures of cities and neighbourhoods. _____
2 They are both students. Larry is 22 and Sergey is 21. _____
3 Craig is a student at Stanford University. _____
4 Contest winners' artwork appears on Google's home page for one day each year. _____
5 Google.com becomes one of the most frequently used websites in the world. _____
6 These languages include Dutch, Chinese and Korean. _____
7 People can explore the world's top museums from their computers. _____
8 It is a verb that means 'to search for something on the internet'. _____

WRITING TASK

Write a narrative paragraph about the history of a business.

PLAN

1 Look back at your timeline and your notes about the company you did research on in the Critical thinking section. Add any new information to your notes. Make sure each letter (a–h) has at least one additional fact.

2 Work with a partner. From the eight events you identified, select the four which you think are most important. Explain to a partner why you selected these four.

3 Write a topic sentence that explains what you are going to write about.

____

____

____

4 Refer to the Task checklist below as you prepare your paragraph.

WRITE A FIRST DRAFT

5 Write a first draft of your paragraph.

REVISE

6 Use the Task checklist to review your paragraph for content and structure.

TASK CHECKLIST	✔
Did you write about the history of a business?	
Did you write about four main facts in time order?	
Did you give the date or time that the events happened?	
Did you add details to the main facts?	

7 Make any necessary changes to your paragraph.

EDIT

8 Use the Language checklist to edit your paragraph for language errors.

LANGUAGE CHECKLIST	✔
Did you use the correct collocations with *business*?	
Did you use the correct forms of the present simple and the past simple?	
Did you use time clauses with *when* correctly?	

9 Make any necessary changes to your paragraph.

OBJECTIVES REVIEW

1 Check your learning objectives for this unit. Write *3*, *2* or *1* for each objective.

3 = very well   2 = well   1 = not so well

I can ...

watch and understand a video about Amazon's fulfilment centre. ______

work out meaning from context. ______

annotate a text. ______

organize events in time order. ______

use the present simple and the past simple. ______

use time clauses with *when* to describe past events. ______

add details to main facts. ______

write a narrative paragraph. ______

2 Use the *Unlock* Digital Workbook for more practice with this unit's learning objectives.

UNLOCK ONLINE

WORDLIST

advertise (v)	goal (n) ⊙	partner (n) ⊙
advice (n) ⊙	hobby (n)	product (n) ⊙
apply (v) ⊙	introduce (v) ⊙	result (n) ⊙
colleague (n)	manager (n) ⊙	run (v) ⊙
customer (n) ⊙	neat (adj)	section (n) ⊙
department (n) ⊙	occupation (n) ⊙	set up (phr v)
employ (v) ⊙	office (n) ⊙	
employee (n) ⊙	organize (v) ⊙	

⊙ = high-frequency words in the Cambridge Academic Corpus

LEARNING OBJECTIVES	IN THIS UNIT YOU WILL ...
Watch and listen	watch and understand a video about a professional gold prospector.
Reading skills	skim a text.
Critical thinking	categorize ideas.
Grammar	use noun phrases with *of*; use modals of necessity.
Academic writing skill	write concluding sentences.
Writing task	write an explanatory paragraph.

UNIT 7

PEOPLE

UNLOCK YOUR KNOWLEDGE

Look at the small photos and answer the questions.

1 What are the names of the people?
2 What did they do to become famous?

PLUS

WATCH AND LISTEN

PREPARING TO WATCH

ACTIVATING YOUR KNOWLEDGE

1 You are going to watch a video about looking for gold. Work with a partner. Discuss the questions.

1 Why do people look for gold?
2 What things are made from gold?
3 What countries is gold found in? Where do people look for it?
4 Do you think finding gold is difficult? Why / Why not?

PREDICTING CONTENT USING VISUALS

2 Work with a partner. Look at the pictures and the glossary. Describe what you can see in each picture.

GLOSSARY

pure (adj) Something that is pure is not mixed with anything else, for example, pure gold, pure water.

prospector (n) a person whose job is looking for gold, oil, etc.

shovel (n) a thing for moving stones, snow, etc.

£20/$100, etc. worth of something (phr) the amount of something that you can buy or sell for £20/$100, etc.

dream job (n phr) the perfect job; the job that you want more than any other

WHILE WATCHING

UNDERSTANDING MAIN IDEAS

3 Watch the video. Write *T* (true) or *F* (false) next to the statements below. Correct the false statements.

_____ 1 Vince's hobby is finding gold.
_____ 2 Vince travels all over the world.
_____ 3 Vince doesn't need a lot of things to look for gold.
_____ 4 Looking for gold is easy.
_____ 5 Some days, Vince doesn't find any gold.
_____ 6 Compared to his office job, Vince earns a lot of money from finding gold.
_____ 7 Vince wants other people to do jobs they enjoy.

UNDERSTANDING DETAIL

4 Watch again. Answer the questions.

1 Who taught Vince how to find gold? ____________________
2 Where did Vince work before? ____________________
3 What is a gold pan? ____________________
4 How many hours a day does Vince work? ____________________
5 What is the most gold Vince finds in a day? ____________________
6 How much money did Vince make in his other job? ____________________
7 How much money does Vince make now? ____________________

MAKING INFERENCES

5 Watch again. Then complete the sentences. Compare your ideas with a partner.

1 Vince left his job because ____________________ .
2 Pieces of gold are often found near each other because ____________________ .
3 Vince has to look for the gold very carefully because ____________________ .
4 These days, Vince feels ____________________ .

DISCUSSION

6 Work in a small group. Discuss the questions.

1 Would you like to try to find some gold? Why / Why not?
2 Is it more important to you to earn a lot of money or to follow your dreams? Why?
3 What is your dream job? Why?

READING

READING 1

PREPARING TO READ

UNDERSTANDING KEY VOCABULARY

1 Read the definitions. Complete the sentences with the words in bold.

blind (adj) not able to see
incredible (adj) impossible or very difficult to believe; amazing
inspire (v) to make other people feel that they want to do something
operation (n) the process when doctors cut your body to repair it or to remove something
respect (v) to like or to have a very good opinion of someone because of their knowledge, achievements, etc.
talent (n) a natural ability to do something well

1 After the ________ on his foot, Alex had to stay in hospital until he could walk on his own.
2 Liz Murray went to Harvard and then became a best-selling author. It is ________ to think that she was homeless only a few years before she went to Harvard.
3 Julia was ________ when she was born. As she could not see, her parents taught her words by putting objects in her hands so she could touch them.
4 Fernanda had a special ________ for playing the piano. She could listen to a song and then play it almost perfectly without any practice.
5 Mahatma Gandhi did a lot of important things for the people of India. I really ________ him and everything he did for people.
6 Having more examples of women as CEOs of businesses will ________ more young girls to reach for similar goals.

SKILLS

Skimming

When you *skim* a text, you read it quickly to find out the general topic. Skimming can help you decide if a text is useful. You can then decide whether to read the text again properly. You do not have to read every word of the text when skimming. Read the title and subtitles. Look at the photos. Notice key words as you look over the text. You can also read the first and last sentence of each paragraph.

SKIMMING

2 Read the blog post opposite quickly. You do not have to read every word. What is the blog post about?

a someone who helped people with cancer
b someone who was blind and trained to be a doctor
c someone who was blind but learnt how to 'see'

INCREDIBLE PEOPLE

About me

My name is Juliet Selby. I write about people that I admire. I write about a different person every week. Read about their amazing lives here!

/2017//Ben Underwood

1 Ben Underwood was a normal teenage boy. He loved playing basketball, riding his bike, listening to music with his friends and playing video games. But in one way, Ben was different from most other teenagers – he was blind. However, Ben had a special **talent**. He didn't have eyes, but he could still 'see'.

2 Ben was born on 26 January 1992. For the first two years of his life, Ben was a happy and healthy baby. He had a normal life, living with his mother and two older brothers in California. However, when Ben was two years old, his life changed. In 1994, he was taken to the hospital because he had problems with his eyes. The doctors looked at his eyes and told his mother the bad news – Ben had cancer[1]. After a few months, he had an **operation** to remove the cancer. The operation was successful and Ben was fine. However, the doctors had to remove his eyes and Ben became **blind**.

3 After his operation, Ben developed an **incredible** talent. When he was three, he learnt how to 'see' buildings with his ears. He listened very carefully and he could hear noises bounce off buildings. The noises told him where the buildings were. Then, when Ben was seven, he learnt to 'click'. He made clicking noises with his mouth and listened for the noises that bounced back from things. In this way, Ben could 'see' where he was and what was around him. This is the same way dolphins see things underwater and bats see in the dark.

4 Scientists and doctors were amazed by Ben's talent. There are only a few blind people in the world who can see like Ben. People **respected** him because of this. He became famous. He was on TV and he travelled to different countries and talked to people about his life. Sadly, when Ben was 16, his cancer came back. He died soon after. However, during Ben's life, he taught people that anything is possible. Many people admired him because he **inspired** them and helped them feel strong. When he died in 2009, over 2,000 people went to his funeral.

[1]**cancer** (n) a serious disease that makes people very sick, because cells in the body grow in ways that are not normal or controlled

WHILE READING

READING FOR MAIN IDEAS

3 Read the blog post again. Write the paragraph number where you can find the information below.

a Ben learnt to 'see' again. Paragraph: _____
b Ben was an ordinary boy, but he could do something amazing. Paragraph: _____
c Ben became a hero for many people. Paragraph: _____
d Ben became ill and lost his eyes. Paragraph: _____

READING FOR DETAIL

4 Read the blog post again and write *T* (true) or *F* (false) next to the statements. Correct the false statements.

_____ 1 Ben liked playing basketball.
____

_____ 2 Ben was just like other teenagers.
____

_____ 3 Ben learnt to 'see' by touching things.
____

_____ 4 Ben couldn't ride a bicycle.
____

_____ 5 Ben had two older brothers.
____

_____ 6 Ben liked listening to music.
____

5 Put the events in Ben's life in the correct order on the timeline.

a Ben learnt how to 'see' buildings with his ears.
b Ben was born.
c Ben learnt how to 'click'.
d Ben's cancer came back.
e Ben had a problem with his eyes.
f Ben died.
g Ben went on TV.

1	2	3	4	5	6	7
_____	_____	_____	_____	_____	_____	_____

READING BETWEEN THE LINES

WORKING OUT MEANING FROM CONTEXT

6 Look at the highlighted words in the text. Then look at the sentence below and circle the word that is a synonym for the word in bold.

I really **admire** her. She's an excellent teacher.

a dislike
b respect
c employ

IDENTIFYING PURPOSE

7 Circle the correct answer.

1 Who do you think wrote the blog?
  a a scientist
  b a journalist
2 Why do you think the author wrote this blog?
  a to teach doctors about cancer
  b to tell people the story of Ben's life

8 Compare your answers in Exercise 8 with a partner. Do you agree or disagree? Which parts of the text helped you answer the question?

DISCUSSION

9 Think of another famous child or teenager and discuss the questions with a partner.

1 What is his/her name? How old is he/she?
2 Why is he/she famous?
3 How is his/her life different from other children's or teenagers' lives? Think about the list below.
   - school
   - hobbies
   - friends
   - home

PLUS

READING 2

PREPARING TO READ

UNDERSTANDING KEY VOCABULARY

1 You are going to read some more blog posts about incredible people. Read the sentences (1–8) and write the words in bold next to the correct definitions (a–h).

1 My mum thinks I'm too young to **look after** my little sister, so a babysitter comes to my house every day.
2 My **former** job was boring because I sat at my computer all day. At my current job, I talk to a lot of customers and I like that much better.
3 Aisha runs at least 16 kilometres every morning to **train** for the upcoming race.
4 It is important for a president to be **honest**. People must be able to trust the person leading their country.
5 People say Terence Tao is one of the most **intelligent** people in the world. He got a PhD at the age of 20 and became a Maths professor at the age of 24.
6 Eugene was **brave** when he ran into a burning house to save an elderly woman. He could have died, but he did it anyway.
7 After five tries, 64-year-old Diana Nyad was finally able to **achieve** her goal of swimming from Cuba to Florida. It took her almost 53 hours to finish the 160-kilometre swim.
8 William graduated from university and then decided to follow his **dream** of opening a restaurant.

a ________ (n) something that you really want to do, be or have in the future
b ________ (phr v) to take care of someone or something by keeping them healthy or in a good condition
c ________ (adj) not showing fear of dangerous or difficult situations
d ________ (adj) before the present time or in the past
e ________ (adj) able to learn and understand things easily; clever
f ________ (v) to prepare for a job, activity or sport by learning skills or by exercise
g ________ (adj) truthful or able to be trusted; not likely to lie, cheat or steal
h ________ (v) to succeed in doing something difficult

PLUS

INCREDIBLE PEOPLE

/Steve Jobs

1 I really admire Steve Jobs, the **former** CEO of Apple. He invented a new kind of technology. Apple technology is very **intelligent**, but it is also easy to use. The products that he made are also really beautiful. Steve Jobs is a good role model[1] because he was an excellent businessman. He worked hard and he created a successful business in IT. I was very sad when he died in October 2011. I respect him because he changed the way people use technology all over the world.

Ahmed Aziz, ____________________

/Mary Evans

2 My mum, Mary Evans, is my role model. I have a very big family, with two brothers and three sisters. My mum worked very hard every day to **look after** us, and she was very busy. She always makes time for everyone and she always listens to me if I have a problem. She gives me advice and she is always right. I have a nephew who is sick and has to go to the hospital a lot. My mum often sleeps at the hospital with him. I really respect her because she always looks after my family and makes sure that we have everything we need.

Mark Evans, ____________________

/Singapore Women's Everest Team

3 My role models are the Singapore Women's Everest Team. In 2009, they became the first all-women team to climb Mount Everest. The team of six young women **trained** for seven years before they climbed the mountain. It was difficult for them to train because Singapore doesn't have any snow or mountains. But they didn't stop, and in the end they **achieved** their goal. They worked hard every day for their **dream**, so I really admire them.

Li Chan, ____________________

/Malala Yousafzai

4 Malala Yousafzai is a **brave** and **honest** young woman. In Pakistan, the Taliban didn't let girls go to school. Malala went anyway. She wrote a blog for the BBC describing the terrible things the Taliban were doing. In 2012, two men came onto her school bus and shot her in the head. Luckily, Malala survived. She gave speeches about the millions of girls around the world who were not allowed to go to school. In 2014, Malala won the Nobel Peace Prize. She donated her $1.1 million prize money to build a school for girls in Pakistan. Malala is a good role model because she is brave, she never gives up, and she tells the truth no matter what.

Jane Kloster, ____________________

[1]**role model** (n) someone you try to behave like because you admire them

WHILE READING

READING FOR MAIN IDEAS

2 Read the blog posts on page 155. Match the sentence halves.

1 Steve Jobs
2 Mary Evans
3 The Singapore Women's Everest Team
4 Malala Yousafzai

a looks after her family.
b fights for girls to go to school.
c invented a new kind of technology.
d climbed a mountain.

READING FOR DETAIL

3 Look at the sentences. There is one mistake in each one. Correct the false information.

1 In 2009, the Singapore Women's Everest team climbed Everest after five years of training.

____

2 Malala Yousafzai donated $1.1 million to build a library in Pakistan.

____

3 Steve Jobs died in June 2011.

____

4 Mark's mother looks after Mark's grandmother in hospital.

____

READING BETWEEN THE LINES

MAKING INFERENCES

4 In the text on page 155, the jobs of the people writing the comments have been removed. Write the jobs of the writers next to their names.

a an explorer
b a teacher
c an IT technician
d a university student

DISCUSSION

SYNTHESIZING

5 Use ideas from Reading 1 and Reading 2 to answer the following questions.

1 What are the different ways in which people can become famous?
2 How can famous people inspire others to do good things?
3 Do you want to be famous? Why / Why not?

LANGUAGE DEVELOPMENT

NOUN PHRASES WITH *OF*

GRAMMAR

You can use the word *of* to join two nouns together and make a noun phrase.

He is the president ***of*** *the country.*

She invented a type ***of*** *technology.*

We write a conclusion at the end ***of*** *an essay.*

1 Match the sentence halves.

1 A chair is	**a** the director of the school.
2 I travel to	**b** the beginning of the day.
3 A camel is	**c** a kind of furniture.
4 Coffee is	**d** a lot of countries.
5 Write your name at	**e** a sort of drink.
6 My teacher is	**f** the top of the page.
7 We eat breakfast at	**g** a type of animal.

2 Put the words in order to make complete sentences.

1 the new leader / She / of / the country / is / .

____

2 of / I met / my brother's / a friend / .

____

3 gave me / of / a piece / My mother / cake / .

____

4 a kind / A dentist / doctor / is / of / .

____

5 of / the former director / is / technology / He / .

____

6 my / is / best friends / Jules / one / of / .

____

7 the day / feel tired / I / in / always / the middle / of / .

____

8 at his school / has / a good / friends / of / Our son / group / .

____

PLUS

ADJECTIVES TO DESCRIBE PEOPLE

3 Are the adjectives in the box positive or negative? Write the words in the correct place in the table.

calm clever confident difficult friendly honest intelligent kind lazy patient reliable selfish sensible shy stupid talented

positive	negative

4 Use adjectives from Exercise 3 to complete the sentences.

1 Luka is very __________ . He always tells the truth.
2 My teacher is always __________ . She is very relaxed and doesn't get worried or angry.
3 She always chats with students in other classes. She's so __________ .
4 She doesn't talk very much. She's really __________ .
5 James hasn't done anything all day. He's so __________ .
6 Ahmed is very __________ . He always comes to work on time and does his job.
7 Ishmael is practical and doesn't do anything stupid. He's very __________ .
8 He is a very __________ driver. He wins every race easily.
9 Don't be so __________ ! Share your toys with your sister.
10 Our daughter is so __________ . She's the best in her class at Maths and Science.

PLUS

WRITING

CRITICAL THINKING

At the end of this unit, you will write an explanatory paragraph. Look at this unit's writing task below.

Who do you think is a good role model? Write a paragraph explaining the qualities that make that person a good role model.

SKILLS

Categorizing ideas

After you collect ideas for your topic, you need to categorize them. This will help you structure your answer in clear paragraphs. For example, writers often use *Venn diagrams* to organize the similarities and differences between people or ideas. In a Venn diagram, write the shared qualities of people or ideas in the overlapping (middle) section of the circles. Write information that is different for each person or idea in the left or right circles.

APPLY

1 Work with a partner. Choose two people from Reading 2 to compare. Complete the Venn diagram to find the shared qualities of the people. Think about adjectives that describe them and the things these people have done.

2 Read the four reasons why the people in Reading 2 are role models. Write the name of the person next to the reason. More than one answer is possible.

a because they are good at sports ____________________
b because they help people ____________________
c because they are intelligent ____________________
d because they were head of a company ____________________

ANALYZE

3 Think of two of your own role models. Write lists of their qualities.

4 Complete the Venn diagram to find the shared qualities of the two role models you chose.

5 Can you think of other reasons that someone might be a role model? Add your reasons to the list.

1 *because they help to change the world*
2 ____________________
3 ____________________
4 ____________________

EVALUATE

6 Choose one of the role models from the Venn diagram in Exercise 4. Why is he or she a good role model?

7 Think of four more things that this person has done that makes him or her a good role model, and add them to the Venn diagram in Exercise 4.

GRAMMAR FOR WRITING

MODALS OF NECESSITY

GRAMMAR

Should, *have to* and *must* express what is required, necessary or strongly suggested.
should = strong suggestion
have to / has to = something is necessary
must = something is necessary or required (very strong)
A role model **should** inspire people.
Role models **have to** set a good example for others.
A role model **must** be kind.

The negative forms are *should not*, *do / does not have to* and *must not*.
should not = strong suggestion not to do something
do / does not have to = something is not necessary
must not = something is forbidden
A good role model **should not** / **must not** be lazy.
People **do not have to** be rich to be good role models.

In academic writing, use the modal *should* or the phrase *it is important to* to say what you believe is the right or best thing to do.
It is important to stay in school.
We **should** spend more time helping others.

1 Which of these things should good role models be or do? Write sentences using *should*, *must*, *have to* or *should not*, *must not*, *do not have to*. Use the phrases in brackets.

Good role models should be sensible.

1 (work hard)

____

2 (be famous)

____

3 (ask others what they need)

____

4 (be patient)

____

5 (be unfriendly to others)

____

6 (be clever)

____

2 Which of these things are important for role models? Choose two of the ideas below and write sentences using *it is important to*. Use the phrases in brackets.

1 (be patient)

___

2 (spend time with your family)

___

3 (learn about other people)

___

4 (get a good education)

___

5 (be reliable)

___

3 Compare and discuss your answers with a partner. Do you agree or disagree? Why?

4 How can people achieve their goals? Write sentences about what each person should or should not do. Use the words in brackets.

1 Hanif wants to open a restaurant. (must)
Hanif must work hard and save a lot of money.

2 Maria wants to be a doctor. (have to)

___

3 Jun wants to be a famous author. (should)

___

4 Thomas wants to save money so he can travel abroad. (should not)

___

5 Jamila wants to get good grades at university. (must not)

___

6 Helen wants to live in a foreign country in the future. (it is important to)

___

ACADEMIC WRITING SKILLS

CONCLUDING SENTENCES

SKILLS

The *concluding sentence* is the last sentence in a paragraph. The concluding sentence gives your opinion and repeats the main idea of the paragraph using different words. Writers sometimes use phrases such as *in conclusion, in summary* or *in short* to begin concluding sentences.

1 Look at the two sentences. Which one is a concluding sentence?

a In summary, I admire my mother because she is kind.
b First, she always look after my brother and me.

2 Underline the phrase in Exercise 1 that shows you it is a concluding sentence.

3 What type of punctuation follows the phrase you underlined?

a a full stop
b a comma

4 Match the topic sentences (1–4) to the concluding sentences (a–d).

Topic sentences

1 I really admire my teacher, Mrs Franklin. ______
2 My parents look after my brother and me. ______
3 Professional footballers have to train every day. ______
4 My uncle is my hero. ______

Concluding sentences

a In conclusion, I admire him a lot.
b In short, it is difficult to compete against other teams if you don't practise.
c In summary, they work hard to make sure we have everything we need.
d In short, I respect her because she works so hard at the school.

PLUS

5 Read the paragraph and circle the best concluding sentence.

Samantha Cristoforetti has been very successful in life so far. She studied Mechanical Engineering in Germany. Then she joined the Air Force in Italy, her home country. She became a captain. In 2009, Samantha became an astronaut. In 2015, she lived in space for almost 200 days. During her time in space, she posted a lot of beautiful pictures and interacted with people on social media.

a In short, Samantha Cristoforetti still has more that she wants to learn.
b In conclusion, Samantha Cristoforetti has accomplished a lot in her life.
c In summary, Samantha Cristoforetti enjoys using social media.

Samantha Cristoforetti

6 Write concluding sentences for the paragraphs.

1 Rachel Chan is a biologist from Argentina. She finished her PhD in Biochemistry in 1988. Then, she studied how severe weather conditions can hurt plants. With other scientists, she invented seeds that can survive during droughts.

___

2 Leonardo da Vinci was an extremely talented man. He was an artist and engineer who drew pictures of bridges and flying machines. He was also interested in studying the human body and comparing it to the bodies of animals. And of course, he created one of the most famous paintings in the world, the Mona Lisa.

___

3 If you want to become the CEO of a company, you must plan ahead. First, you should study hard at school and get good grades. Next, you should apply to well-known business schools. Then, try to get a job at a company that has a lot of opportunities for you to learn and grow. You will have to work hard, but one day you might get your dream job.

___

WRITING TASK

Who do you think is a good role model? Why? Write a paragraph explaining the qualities that make that person a good role model.

PLAN

1 Write a topic sentence to introduce the person you chose and explain why you think he or she is a good role model.

... is a good role model because ...

____

____

2 Look at the Venn diagram you made in Exercise 4 of the Critical thinking section on page 160. Use the shared qualities of the two people as examples of what makes a person a good role model. Write the qualities and examples in the order you will write about them in your paragraph. What are some of the qualities that are special for the person you chose?

1 ____

____

2 ____

____

3 ____

____

4 ____

____

3 Write a concluding sentence that repeats your main idea in different words. Use phrases like *in conclusion*, *in summary* or *in short* to show that this is the concluding sentence.

____

____

4 Refer to the Task checklist on page 166 as you prepare your paragraph.

WRITE A FIRST DRAFT

5 Write the first draft of your paragraph.

REVISE

6 Use the Task checklist to review your paragraph for content and structure.

TASK CHECKLIST	✔
Did you write about your role model?	
Did you write about why the person is your role model?	
Does your paragraph have a topic sentence, supporting sentences and a concluding sentence?	
Does your concluding sentence give your opinion and repeat the main idea of the paragraph?	

7 Make any necessary changes to your paragraph.

EDIT

8 Use the Language checklist to edit your paragraph for language errors.

LANGUAGE CHECKLIST	✔
Did you use noun phrases with *of* correctly?	
Did you use adjectives to describe people correctly?	
Did you use *should*, *have to* and *must* correctly?	
Did you use *it is important to* correctly?	

9 Make any necessary changes to your paragraph.

OBJECTIVES REVIEW

1 Check your learning objectives for this unit. Write *3*, *2* or *1* for each objective.

3 = very well 2 = well 1 = not so well

I can …

watch and understand a video about a professional gold prospector. _____

skim a text. _____

categorize ideas. _____

use noun phrases with *of*. _____

use modals of necessity. _____

write concluding sentences. _____

write an explanatory paragraph. _____

2 Use the *Unlock* Digital Workbook for more practice with this unit's learning objectives.

UNLOCK ONLINE

WORDLIST

achieve (v) ⊙	honest (adj) ⊙	respect (v) ⊙
blind (adj) ⊙	incredible (adj)	selfish (adj)
brave (adj)	inspire (v)	sensible (adj) ⊙
calm (adj)	intelligent (adj) ⊙	shy (adj)
clever (adj)	kind (adj) ⊙	stupid (adj)
confident (adj) ⊙	lazy (adj) ⊙	talent (n)
difficult (adj) ⊙	look after (v)	talented (adj)
dream (n) ⊙	operation (n) ⊙	train (v) ⊙
former (adj) ⊙	patient (adj) ⊙	
friendly (adj) ⊙	reliable (adj) ⊙	

⊙ = high-frequency words in the Cambridge Academic Corpus

LEARNING OBJECTIVES	IN THIS UNIT YOU WILL ...
Watch and listen	watch and understand a video about going to the International Space Station.
Reading skill	identify the author's purpose.
Critical thinking	evaluate arguments.
Grammar	use *that* clauses in complex sentences; use infinitives of purpose; use *because* and *so*.
Academic writing skill	organize an essay.
Writing task	complete an opinion essay.

THE UNIVERSE

UNIT 8

UNLOCK YOUR KNOWLEDGE

Look at the photo and answer the questions.

1 What is the person doing? Would you like to try this work? Why / Why not?

2 Why do governments send people to space?

3 Would you like to travel to space? Why / Why not?

PLUS

WATCH AND LISTEN

PREPARING TO WATCH

ACTIVATING YOUR KNOWLEDGE

1 Work with a partner and answer the questions.

1 How do people usually get to work when they live far from their workplace?
2 Why might people live far from their workplace?
3 What are some unusual offices or workplaces?

USING YOUR KNOWLEDGE

2 You are going to watch a video about a woman who travelled to space for work. Write five adjectives and five nouns to describe a trip to space.

Adjectives: ________, ________, ________, ________, ________
Nouns: ________, ________, ________, ________, ________

GLOSSARY

astronaut (n) someone who travels to and works in space

International Space Station (n) the name of an international spacecraft where astronauts work on projects

rocket (n) a vehicle for travelling to space

capsule (n) the part of the rocket where the astronauts are

cosmonaut (n) an astronaut from Russia

blast off (phr v) to leave the ground; for example, when a spacecraft or rocket blasts off, it leaves the ground.

WHILE WATCHING

UNDERSTANDING MAIN IDEAS

3 Watch the video. Answer the questions.

1 What does Sunita Williams do?

____

2 What is the name of her office in space?

____

3 How did she get there?

____

4 What was not a problem when she went there?

____

5 What took longer, her trip to space or her drive to work?

____

UNDERSTANDING DETAIL

4 Watch again. Complete the sentences with the correct numbers.

1 It takes Sunita Williams _____ minutes to drive to the office.
2 She drives her car _____ miles to the office in Houston, Texas.
3 She spent _____ months in space.
4 The trip to space was _____ miles, straight up.
5 The trip took _____ minutes.

5 Correct the mistakes in the student's notes. Compare your answers with a partner.

1 The rocket is American.

2 The trip took double the time it takes her to drive to work.

3 She travelled in a big capsule.

4 She went with a Russian cosmonaut and a Korean astronaut.

5 They rode the elevator to the bottom.

DISCUSSION

6 Work with a partner. Discuss the questions. Explain your answers.

1 What are the dangers of travelling to space?
2 What kind of person works in space?
3 What is 'space tourism'? How do you feel about it?

READING

READING 1

PREPARING TO READ

UNDERSTANDING KEY VOCABULARY

1 Read the sentences (1–7). Write the correct form of the words in bold next to the definitions (a–g).

1 Mariam loves to **explore** new places. Her dream is to go into space.
2 There were many **advances** in science and medicine during the last century. The speed of change was amazing.
3 Astronauts have not set foot **beyond** the moon, but one day soon they may go to planets that are farther away.
4 It is important for an **entrepreneur** to understand that they might lose all of their money if their business fails.
5 The rocket **crashed** when it was landing. Luckily, the people inside were not hurt.
6 Tesla is a **private** company. The government does not run it.
7 Some people don't think we should use **public** money, like taxes, to pay for space travel. They think companies should pay for it.

a ____________ (n) someone who starts their own business
b ____________ (n) progress in the development or improvement of something
c ____________ (adj) related to money or services controlled or supplied by a person or a company and not by the government
d ____________ (v) to travel to a new place to learn about it
e ____________ (prep) on the farther side of; at a farther distance than
f ____________ (v) to hit something by accident, especially in a vehicle
g ____________ (adj) related to money or services controlled or supplied by the government and not by a person or a company

USING YOUR KNOWLEDGE

2 You are going to read an article about space travel. Before you read, discuss the questions with a partner.

1 Who pays for space exploration?
2 Do you think people will ever go on holiday in space? Why / Why not?

NEWS SCIENCE DISCOVERIES TECHNOLOGY EDUCATION BLOGS COMMUNITY

The rise of commercial[1] space travel

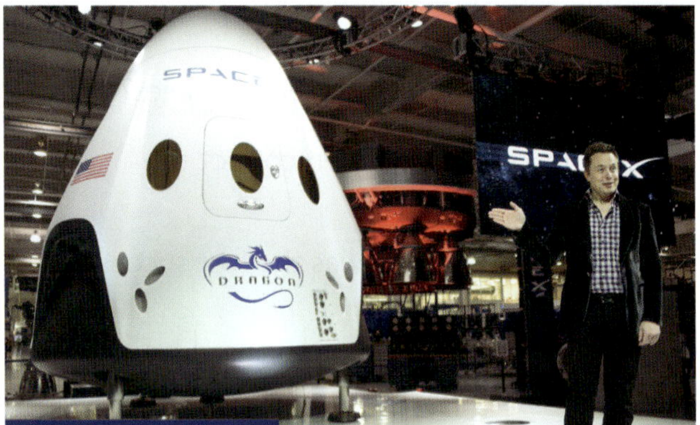

Elon Musk and *Dragon*

1 In 1957, the Soviet Union sent *Sputnik I* into space. It was the first successful spacecraft to orbit[2] the Earth, and it started the time period known as the Space Age. A short time later in the US, the National Aeronautics Space Administration (NASA) successfully sent another spacecraft, *Explorer I*, into space. In the years that followed, incredible **advances** were made. Astronauts orbited the Earth and men walked on the moon. The world, it seemed, wanted to learn what was **beyond** Earth.

2 Today, space exploration continues, and governments still compete with one another to make new discoveries. In 2012, NASA landed its unmanned[3] spacecraft *Curiosity* on Mars in order to collect information about the planet. In 2016, Europe and Russia worked together and sent a spacecraft to Mars. China and India are also working on similar projects. However, there has been one big change: **private** companies, instead of **public** government organizations, are entering the Space Race[4].

3 SpaceX has been very successful in commercial space travel. They designed the spacecraft *Dragon* in order to deliver supplies to the International Space Station (ISS). In 2012, *Dragon* was the first commercial spacecraft in history to do that. Elon Musk, the man who started the company, has dreams that go beyond making deliveries. He hopes that SpaceX will be able to send people to Mars by 2025.

4 Another **entrepreneur** who supports commercial space travel is Sir Richard Branson. He started a private company called Virgin Galactic. Their goal is to open space travel to everyone. The company has sold almost 700 future trips to space, at the high cost of $250,000 per person. Those future space tourists come from countries all over the world and are all different ages.

5 Private companies are lucky in one way. They don't have to wait for money from the government like NASA does. However, that doesn't mean that setbacks[5] and accidents don't happen. In 2014, Virgin Galactic's *VSS Enterprise* **crashed** in the Mojave Desert in the US during a test flight. The 39-year-old pilot, Michael Alsbury, was killed. In 2016, a SpaceX spacecraft that was going to the ISS exploded on the launch pad in Cape Canaveral, Florida. No one was hurt, but important supplies were lost.

6 The race to **explore** the universe continues and many private companies are competing. Some of those companies want to take people to the moon and back someday. Others want to take people to Mars. The possibilities are endless. Maybe in our lifetime, those dreams will come true.

Sir Richard Branson and a Virgin Galactic spacecraft

[1]**commercial** (adj) with the purpose of making money
[2]**orbit** (v) to travel around a planet or star
[3]**unmanned** (adj) without people to operate something
[4]**Space Race** (n) the competition between countries to make advances in the field of space exploration
[5]**setbacks** (n) problems that make something happen later or more slowly than it should

WHILE READING

READING FOR MAIN IDEAS

3 Read the text on page 173 and answer the questions.

1 What is the Space Age?
2 What are countries competing with one another for?
3 What are some goals of future space travel?
4 What is one difference between public and private companies?

READING FOR DETAIL

4 Read the statements. Write *T* (true) or *F* (false). Then correct the false statements.

_____ 1 NASA sent *Sputnik I* into space, and it was the first successful spacecraft to orbit the Earth.
_____ 2 Entrepreneurs like Elon Musk and Sir Richard Branson have to wait for government money in order to build new spacecraft.
_____ 3 In 2016, a SpaceX spacecraft exploded in Cape Canaveral, Florida, and killed its pilot.
_____ 4 Virgin Galactic has sold nearly 700 future trips to space.
_____ 5 The first commercial spacecraft to deliver goods to the International Space Station was called *Dragon*.

READING BETWEEN THE LINES

SKILLS

Identifying the author's purpose

Authors write in order to inform, explain, entertain or persuade readers. The author's purpose may be understood by his or her use of key words, tone and language in the text. Good readers identify why a text was written. The author's purpose may be stated clearly in the text, or it may have to be inferred.

IDENTIFYING PURPOSE

5 Read the text on page 173 again. Circle the correct answers.

1 The purpose of the text is to ...
   a persuade readers that commercial space travel is necessary.
   b inform readers about the advances in commercial space travel.
   c entertain readers about the possibility of life on Mars.
2 You could find the text in ...
   a a magazine.
   b a textbook.
   c a science fiction novel.
3 The author is ...
   a analyzing commercial space travel.
   b describing commercial space travel.
   c questioning the benefits of commercial space travel.

DISCUSSION

6 Discuss the questions with a partner.

1 Would you pay a lot of money to be a space tourist? Why / Why not?
2 Why might some people want to leave Earth and live on Mars?

READING 2

PREPARING TO READ

UNDERSTANDING KEY VOCABULARY

1 You are going to read about life on other planets. Before you read, circle the best definition (a or b) for each word in bold.

1 I often **wonder** if people will travel to Mars one day. Maybe NASA will send someone there in the next 10 or 15 years.
  a think about something and try to understand it
  b not believe something
2 My essay is weak because I didn't **support** my ideas with expert opinions. I should find more research to add to my essay.
  a think of more topics to write about
  b help show that something is true
3 A lot of **evidence** shows that Mars once had flowing water.
  a opinions that people have about a topic
  b something that makes you believe something is true
4 Scientists have been studying space for many years. Some think there is life on other planets, but no one can **prove** it.
  a show that something is true
  b ask questions about something
5 Life can't **exist** without air and water. For that reason, Earth is the perfect planet for life.
  a be real, alive or present
  b change and improve
6 Because it was so difficult, Elise thought it was **unlikely** that she would pass her Astronomy exam.
  a expected to happen; probable
  b not expected to happen; not probable
7 Astronauts have to train a lot in order to prepare for the **conditions** they'll face in space, such as very hot and very cold temperatures.
  a the location of something
  b the situation in which people live, work or do things
8 On **particular** nights, you can see the brightest planets when you look at the sky. That only happens when the sky is clear.
  a used to talk about one thing or person and not others
  b many different things or people, not just one

PLUS

SKIMMING

2 Skim the text on page 177. What type of text is it?

a a story
b an essay
c a newspaper article

WHILE READING

READING FOR MAIN IDEAS

3 Read the text and write the number of the paragraph (1–4) where the author mentions each idea (a–d).

a There is not enough evidence to prove that Kepler 22b has life. Paragraph: ______
b Earth is the only planet with the right conditions for life. Paragraph: ______
c There are arguments for and against the idea that life exists on other planets. Paragraph: ______
d It is unlikely that there is life on another planet, because the conditions for life to exist are too particular. Paragraph: ______

READING FOR DETAIL

4 Answer the questions, using the information in the text.

1 How many solar systems are there in the universe?
____
2 What is the name of the telescope that discovers new planets?
____
3 What is Kepler 22b? ______________________
4 Which university wrote a report saying that it is unlikely that there is life on other planets? ______________________
5 What does the report say we need before we can know if there is life on other planets? ______________________

Kepler 22b

Life on other planets

1 For many years, people have **wondered** whether we are the only living things in the universe. Some scientists believe that there must be life on other planets because the universe is so big. However, it is **unlikely** that there is life on other planets because planets need a very specific environment for life to start. In the end, there are no facts that **support** the idea of life on other planets.

2 First of all, it is true that the universe is huge. It has billions of stars and thousands of solar systems. As of 2016, experts using the very powerful Kepler telescope[1] have found more than 2,300 planets in orbit around stars. A lot of these planets are similar to Earth. In fact, a number of scientists believe that one of these planets, named Kepler 22b, has the right **conditions** – the right atmosphere[2] and temperature – to support life. However, there is no **evidence** that there is life on Kepler 22b. Experts with the best technology can see no signs of life there. Until there is hard evidence, we cannot use Kepler 22b to support the idea of life on other planets.

3 A planet needs very **particular** conditions to support life. A planet with life would need to have water, the right temperature and the right mix of chemicals in the atmosphere. Earth has the perfect conditions for life, and it is very unlikely that another planet has exactly the same environment as Earth. In addition, although scientists believe that life might **exist** on other planets, they have never found evidence to **prove** it. A recent report from Princeton University suggests that it is highly unlikely that there is life on other planets. The researchers believe that we don't have enough scientific evidence to decide if there is life on other planets. They say that just because conditions similar to Earth exist on other planets, it doesn't mean that life exists there.

4 In conclusion, I do not believe that there is life on other planets. Although the universe is very big, a planet with life needs very special conditions. Earth has exactly the right conditions for life. It is not too hot or too cold. It has water, air and the right chemicals. I do not think that any other planets could have exactly the same conditions as Earth. Therefore, I do not think that there could be life on other planets.

[1]**telescope** (n) a piece of equipment, in the shape of a tube, that makes things that are far away look bigger or nearer
[2]**atmosphere** (n) the layer of gases around a planet

READING BETWEEN THE LINES

MAKING INFERENCES

5 Why do you think Kepler 22b was given its name?

DISTINGUISHING FACT FROM OPINION

6 Read the sentences from the text. Which are facts and which are opinions? Write *F* (fact) or *O* (opinion).

1 There must be life on other planets. _____
2 The universe has billions of stars and thousands of solar systems. _____
3 It is highly unlikely that there is life on other planets. _____
4 A planet needs very particular conditions to support life. _____

IDENTIFYING PURPOSE

7 Read the questions (1–3) and circle the correct answers (a–c).

1 What is the author's main purpose?
  a to entertain readers
  b to make readers agree with his or her opinion
  c to inform readers
2 What does the author believe?
  a The universe is so big that there must be life on other planets.
  b Life probably doesn't exist on other planets.
  c Life most likely exists on other planets; we just have to find it.
3 Why does the author include information from a recent report from Princeton University?
  a to prove that experts agree with his or her opinion
  b to show that there are two sides to the argument
  c to prove that life exists on other planets

DISCUSSION

8 Space exploration has led to many inventions. With a partner, rank these inventions in order of importance from *1* (the most important) to *7* (the least important).

a microcomputers _____
b GPS navigation _____
c satellite TV _____
d weather forecasts _____
e electric cars _____
f robotic arms _____
g freeze-dried food _____

SYNTHESIZING

9 Use information from Reading 1 and Reading 2 to answer the questions.

1 Will private companies make it possible for tourists to go to the moon or to explore planets like Mars or Kepler 22b? Why / Why not?
2 Will private companies help us learn more about other planets and their environments? Why / Why not?

PLUS

LANGUAGE DEVELOPMENT

GIVING EVIDENCE AND SUPPORTING AN ARGUMENT

VOCABULARY

In an essay, good writers support their arguments with evidence. You can use the nouns *research, study, expert* and *report* to support arguments. You can use verbs like *think* or *believe* for a person, and *show* or *suggest* for a piece of work, e.g. a study or report.

1 Write the nouns from the box next to the correct definitions. One definition has two correct answers.

study	report	research	expert

1 __________ (n) someone who has a lot of skill in something or a lot of knowledge about something
2 __________ / __________ (n) a document that tells us about a subject in detail
3 __________ (n) the study of a subject to discover new information

2 Complete the sentences with the correct verbs from the box. More than one answer is possible.

think	believe	show	suggest

1 Experts __________ that the moon is too cold for people to live there.
2 Studies __________ that there are over 200 billion stars in the Milky Way galaxy.
3 Scientists __________ that we need to study space.
4 Reports __________ that parts of Mars were once covered in ice.
5 Research __________ that there could be 50 billion planets in our galaxy.

PLUS

the Milky Way

WRITING

CRITICAL THINKING

At the end of this unit, you will complete an opinion essay. Look at this unit's writing task below.

> Should governments spend more money on space exploration?
> Give reasons and examples to support your opinion.

ANALYZE

1 With a partner, look back at paragraph 1 of Reading 2 on page 177. What is the author's main argument?

____

2 What are the reasons the author gives to support his or her argument? Look at paragraphs 2 and 3.

Paragraph 2: ____

____

____

____

Paragraph 3: ____

____

____

____

3 Read the opinions about funding for space exploration on page 181. Notice that the opinions come from different people and organizations. Underline the sentence or sentences that show the writer's opinion about funding space travel.

a

Source: The International Space Agency

Governments around the world should spend more money on space programmes. The International Space Station (ISS) is a good example why. The ISS has existed since 1998 and brings together many countries. Astronauts live in space and take part in important experiments. In 2015, Russia and the US sent astronauts to live on the ISS for one year to observe the effects of space on the human body. Long-term journeys, such as travelling to Mars, will never happen without this important research. The ISS cost about $100 billion and one country could not pay for that on its own. International space exploration proves that countries can work together. It represents the spirit of partnership. With so much war in the world, governments should spend more money on things they can achieve together. Maybe that will help bring peace.

b

Source: A newspaper editorial

The US has spent more than $16 billion per year on its space programme since 1958. For a long time, the cost was worth it because of the advances made in science and technology. However, space travel is not only expensive, but it is also dangerous. Astronauts have been killed as recently as 2014. Also, we shouldn't waste natural resources on building new spacecraft. More money should be spent on people who need clean water and food, on access to education and on medical research. For example, a Japanese study found that a drug made from sea sponges helps treat several types of cancer. And yet 90% of the Earth's oceans are still unexplored. The ocean is a valuable resource. Governments should spend more money on ocean exploration than on space exploration.

c

Source: A government agency

Uncovering the mysteries of space is a huge task that should continue to be funded. Imagine the discoveries and advances in technology that will be made as countries go farther and farther into space, especially in the race to be the first to Mars. Furthermore, people may need to live on Mars someday because Earth will become too crowded and too hot. Also, asking questions about the universe encourages young people to study Science and Engineering, which is a huge benefit to society. Medical advances are also made as a result of sending humans to space. For example, when astronauts are in space, their bones become weaker and more likely to break. Many elderly people also have weak bones. Drugs that can help elderly people can be tested on astronauts in space. Research done in space can improve life on Earth. Governments should absolutely spend more money on space programmes.

4 Complete the T-chart with the reasons and evidence the writers give for and against funding space exploration. List the source (a, b or c) next to each reason you list.

for	against
Astronauts take part in important experiments (a)	

SKILLS

Evaluating arguments

It is important to think about how good the different arguments about a topic are. Some arguments are stronger than others. *Evaluate* by deciding how strong an argument is. Is there strong evidence to support the argument? Opinions must be supported by evidence (reasons and examples) to produce a strong argument. This can help you decide which arguments to include in an essay.

EVALUATE

5 Circle the arguments in the T-chart that you think are the strongest. Then discuss with a partner why you think these arguments are the strongest.

6 Work with a partner. Think of evidence and examples for the arguments you chose in Exercise 5.

7 Which opinion do you agree with most? Explain why.

a Governments should spend more money on exploring space.

b Governments should not spend more money on exploring space.

GRAMMAR FOR WRITING

THAT CLAUSES IN COMPLEX SENTENCES

GRAMMAR

Good writers use a variety of sentence structures to make their writing interesting. Writers should use simple, compound and complex sentences. In some complex sentences, *that* clauses are used to give supporting evidence.

That clauses begin with *that* and have their own subject and verb.

main clause (*subject* … *verb*) | *that clause* (*subject* … *verb*)

NASA scientists learnt **that human bones can become weaker in space.**

In conversation and informal writing, *that* is often omitted. In formal, academic writing, use *that*.

main clause (*subject* … *verb*) | *that clause* (*subject* … *verb*)

Many people are sure **they will travel to Mars someday**. *(informal)*

main clause (*subject* … *verb*) | *that clause* (*subject* … *verb*)

Many people are sure **that they will travel to Mars someday**. *(formal)*

You can use reporting verbs (*explain*, *think*, *show*, *say*, *believe*, *hope*, *doubt*, *claim*, *state*, *suggest*) in the main clause to give supporting evidence and examples for an argument. For example:

Some people think + *that* clause.
Studies show + *that* clause.
Scientists believe + *that* clause.
Some experts suggest + *that* clause.

There must be life on other planets. → **Some scientists believe** that there must be life on other planets.

Travelling to space is dangerous. → **Some people think** that travelling to space is dangerous.

Oceans are a valuable resource. → **Studies show** that oceans are a valuable resource.

Humans will have to live on another planet someday. → **Some experts suggest** that humans will have to live on another planet someday.

Note: It is not necessary to use a comma before *that*.

1 Put the words in order to make complex sentences with *that* clauses.

1 we could live / by 2050 / on the moon / Scientists believe that / .

____

2 not a planet / Reports show that / is / Pluto / .

____

3 a good way / to learn about science / TV programmes / are / Some people think that / .

____

4 life / on other planets / Studies suggest that / could exist / .

____

2 Rewrite the quotations as complex sentences with reporting verbs and *that* clauses. The first one has been done for you as an example.

1 'SpaceX built *Dragon* in order to deliver supplies to the International Space Station.' – Elon Musk
Elon Musk said that SpaceX built *Dragon* in order to deliver supplies to the International Space Station.

2 'Regular people should have the opportunity to travel in space.' – Sir Richard Branson

3 'We doubt that alien life exists.' – Researchers at Princeton University

4 'The Kepler telescope looks for liveable planets beyond Earth.' – NASA

PLUS

INFINITIVES OF PURPOSE

GRAMMAR

You can use *in order to* + the infinitive to express a purpose, or why something is done. Think of it as answering a 'Why?' question.

You can use *to* + the infinitive alone. *In order to* + the infinitive is more formal. *To* + the infinitive is more informal.

NASA sent robots to Mars **(in order) to find** water.
SpaceX designed *Dragon* **(in order) to deliver** supplies.

3 Match the sentence halves.

1 We build rockets
2 We sent the International Space Station into space
3 We want to land on the moon

a (in order) to explore it in more detail.
b (in order) to send people into space.
c (in order) to find out if people could live in space.

4 Complete the sentence in three different ways, using infinitives.

1 We explore space (in order) ______________________________ .
2 We explore space (in order) ______________________________ .
3 We explore space (in order) ______________________________ .

BECAUSE AND *SO*

GRAMMAR

Because and *so* express causes and effects. A clause that shows the cause of or reason of an action follows *because*. A clause that shows the effect or result of an action follows *so*. Use *because* and *so* to join two clauses. Each clause must have a subject and a verb. Put a comma before *so*.

reason: I want to be an astronaut. result: I'm studying Computer Science.

→ I'm studying Computer Science **because** I want to be an astronaut.

→ I want to be an astronaut, **so** I'm studying Computer Science.

reason: Governments spend too much money on space exploration.
result: Governments don't have enough money for medical research.

→ Governments don't have enough money for medical research **because** they spend too much money on space exploration.

→ Governments spend too much money on space exploration, **so** they don't have enough money for medical research.

5 Match the sentences in column A to the sentences in column B. The first one has been done for you as an example.

A ________	B ________
1 I read about different planets.	a I want to design spaceships.
2 I'm studying Mars.	b I like to look at the stars and planets.
3 I study Engineering.	c I want to be an entrepreneur.
4 I bought a telescope.	d I want to explore new places.
5 I study Business.	e I want to learn more about space.

6 Write *reason* and *result* in the gaps (A or B) above the columns to show which sentences are the reason sentences and which are the result sentences.

7 Look at the sentences below with *because* and *so*. Underline the reason sentence and circle the result sentence.

1 I'm studying Maths and Physics *because* I want to be an engineer.
2 I want to be an engineer, *so* I'm studying Maths and Physics.

8 Join each pair of sentences in Exercise 5 to make one sentence. Write *because* or *so*. The first one has been done for you as an example.

1 I read about different planets because I want to learn more about space.
2 ________________________________
3 ________________________________
4 ________________________________
5 ________________________________

ACADEMIC WRITING SKILLS

ESSAY ORGANIZATION

SKILLS

An essay is a group of paragraphs about the same topic. Essays are common in academic writing. An essay responds to an essay question.

An essay has an *introductory paragraph*, one or more *main body paragraphs* and a *concluding paragraph*.

introductory paragraph: The introductory paragraph gives background information about a topic. Background information can be general information about the topic, historical information or a story that helps readers understand why the topic is important. The last sentence of the introductory paragraph is the **thesis statement**. This tells the reader what the essay will be about. It is similar to a topic sentence for a paragraph and it includes the writer's point of view. It also says what the main body paragraphs will discuss.

main body paragraphs: Each main body paragraph has a topic sentence and supporting sentences. Supporting sentences include facts, reasons and examples that support the essay's ideas.

concluding paragraph: The concluding paragraph retells or summarizes the main points in the essay. The writer gives his or her opinion again.

1 Use the words from the box to complete the summary about the correct order of paragraphs in an essay.

middle	last	first	one

PLUS

The introductory paragraph is the (1)__________ paragraph in an essay. The body is the (2)__________ paragraph or set of paragraphs of the essay. The body can be (3)__________ paragraph or many paragraphs. The concluding paragraph is the (4)__________ paragraph in an essay.

2 Look at the essay in Reading 2 again on page 177. Follow the instructions.

1 In the introductory paragraph, circle the background information about the topic. Underline the thesis statement.
2 In the main body paragraphs, highlight the facts, reasons and examples that support the argument.
3 In the concluding paragraph, circle the phrases that retell the main points in the essay. Underline the writer's opinion.

WRITING TASK

Should governments spend more money on space exploration?
Give reasons and examples to support your opinion.

PLAN

1 Look at the essay planner below and answer the questions.

a In which paragraphs should you give support for your opinion?
b In which paragraph should you write your conclusion?
c In which paragraphs should you include your opinion about the topic?
d Complete the thesis statement in the first paragraph of the essay planner. Then circle *should* or *should not* in the concluding paragraph on page 188 to show your opinion. Then summarize your main points.

2 Refer to the Task checklist on page 188 as you prepare your essay.

WRITE A FIRST DRAFT

3 Use your ideas from the Critical thinking section to complete the essay planner.

1 Space exploration is very expensive. Between 1981 and 2011, the US government spent $192 billion on its space programme. Many people believe that space exploration is a waste of money. However, other people think that it is an important and exciting project and that we should spend money on it. In my opinion, ______________________________
____
______________________________.

2 ______________________________
____
____
____
____
____

3 ______________________________
____
____
____
____
____

4 In conclusion, I think that governments **should** / **should not** spend money on space exploration. ____

____

____

____

____

REVISE

4 Use the Task checklist to review your essay for content and structure.

TASK CHECKLIST	✔
Did you include arguments for or against governments spending money on space exploration?	
Did you write a thesis statement that tells what the essay is about and gives your point of view?	
Did you use evidence and examples to support your arguments?	
Did you summarize your main points and include your own opinion in the concluding paragraph?	

5 Make any necessary changes to your essay.

EDIT

6 Use the Language checklist to edit your essay for language errors.

LANGUAGE CHECKLIST	✔
Did you use vocabulary to give evidence and support arguments?	
Did you use infinitives of purpose correctly?	
Did you use *that* clauses in complex sentences to give evidence and supporting details?	

7 Make any necessary changes to your essay.

OBJECTIVES REVIEW

1 Check your learning objectives for this unit. Write *3*, *2* or *1* for each objective.

3 = very well 2 = well 1 = not so well

I can ...

watch and understand a video about going to the International Space Station.	_____
identify the author's purpose.	_____
evaluate arguments.	_____
use *that* clauses in complex sentences.	_____
use infinitives of purpose.	_____
use *because* and *so*.	_____
organize an essay.	_____
complete an opinion essay.	_____

2 Use the *Unlock* Digital Workbook for more practice with this unit's learning objectives.

UNLOCK ONLINE

WORDLIST

advance (n) ⊙	exist (v) ⊙	research (n) ⊙
believe (v)	explore (v) ⊙	study (n) ⊙
beyond (prep) ⊙	particular (adj) ⊙	suggest (v) ⊙
conditions (n) ⊙	private (adj) ⊙	support (v) ⊙
crash (v)	prove (v) ⊙	unlikely (adj) ⊙
entrepreneur (n)	public (adj) ⊙	wonder (v) ⊙
evidence (n) ⊙	report (n) ⊙	

⊙ = high-frequency words in the Cambridge Academic Corpus

GLOSSARY

⊙ = high-frequency words in the Cambridge Academic Corpus

Vocabulary	Pronunciation	Part of speech	Definition
UNIT 1			
area ⊙	/ˈeəriə/	(n)	a region or part of a larger place, like a country or city
beautiful	/ˈbjuːtɪfəl/	(adj)	very attractive
boring	/ˈbɔːrɪŋ/	(adj)	not interesting or exciting
capital ⊙	/ˈkæpɪtəl/	(n)	the most important city in a country or state; where the government is
cheap ⊙	/tʃiːp/	(adj)	not expensive, or costs less than usual
city centre	/ˈsɪti ˈsentə/	(n)	the main or central part of a city
clean ⊙	/kliːn/	(adj)	not dirty
countryside ⊙	/ˈkʌntrɪsaɪd/	(n)	land that is not in towns or cities and may have farms and fields
expensive ⊙	/ɪkˈspensɪv/	(adj)	costs a lot of money; not cheap
expert ⊙	/ˈekspɜːt/	(n)	someone who has a lot of skill in or a lot of knowledge about something
interesting ⊙	/ˈɪntrəstɪŋ/	(adj)	Someone or something that is interesting keeps your attention because they, or it, are unusual, exciting or have lots of ideas.
local ⊙	/ˈləʊkəl/	(adj)	relating to a particular area, city or town
modern ⊙	/ˈmɒdən/	(adj)	designed and made using the most recent ideas and methods
noisy ⊙	/ˈnɔɪzi/	(adj)	loud; makes a lot of noise

Vocabulary	Pronunciation	Part of speech	Definition
opportunity	/ˌɒpə'tjuːnəti/	(n)	a chance to do or experience something good
polluted	/pə'luːtəd/	(adj)	damaged or dirty because of harmful materials or waste
pollution	/pə'luːʃən/	(n)	damage caused to water, air and land by harmful materials or waste
population	/ˌpɒpjə'leɪʃən/	(n)	the number of people living in a place
quiet	/kwaɪət/	(adj)	makes little or no noise
traffic	/'træfɪk/	(n)	the cars, trucks and other vehicles using a road
ugly	/'ʌgli/	(adj)	unpleasant to look at
UNIT 2			
activity	/æk'tɪvəti/	(n)	something you do for fun
celebrate	/'seləbreɪt/	(v)	to do something enjoyable because it is a special day
culture	/'kʌltʃə/	(n)	the habits, traditions and beliefs of a country or group of people
fireworks	/'faɪəwɜːks/	(n)	small objects that explode to make a loud noise and bright colours in the night sky
gift	/gɪft/	(n)	something that you give to someone, usually on a special day
highlight	/'haɪlaɪt/	(n)	most enjoyable part
history	/'hɪstəri/	(n)	events that happened in the past
lucky	/'lʌki/	(adj)	having good things happen to you

Vocabulary	Pronunciation	Part of speech	Definition
popular	/ˈpɒpjələ/	(adj)	liked by many people
take part	/teɪk pɑːt/	(phr v)	do an activity with other people
traditional	/trəˈdɪʃənəl/	(adj)	following the ways of behaving or doing things that have continued in a group of people for a long time
visitor	/ˈvɪzɪtə/	(n)	someone who goes to see a person or a place

UNIT 3

Vocabulary	Pronunciation	Part of speech	Definition
advert	/ˈædvɜːt/	(n)	a picture, short film, etc. that tells people about something they can buy
affect	/əˈfekt/	(v)	to influence someone or something; to cause change
collect	/kəˈlekt/	(v)	to get things from different places and bring them together
computer program	/kəmˈpjuːtə ˈprəʊgræm/	(n)	a set of instructions that you put into a computer to make it do something
creative	/kriˈeɪtɪv/	(adj)	good at thinking of new ideas or creating new and unusual things
download	/ˌdaʊnˈləʊd/	(v)	to copy programs, music or other information electronically from the internet to your device (e.g. a computer)
educational	/ˌedʒuˈkeɪʃənəl/	(adj)	providing or relating to teaching and learning
email address	/ˈiːmeɪl əˈdres/	(n)	a series of letters, numbers and symbols used to send and receive email

Vocabulary	Pronunciation	Part of speech	Definition
free	/friː/	(adj)	costing no money
imagination	/ɪˌmædʒɪˈneɪʃən/	(n)	the part of your mind that creates ideas or pictures of things that are not real or that you have not seen
improve	/ɪmˈpruːv/	(v)	to get better or to make something better
interest	/ˈɪntrəst/	(n)	something you enjoy doing or learning about
keyboard	/ˈkiːbɔːd/	(n)	a set of keys on a computer that you press to make it work
record	/rɪˈkɔːd/	(v)	to store sounds, pictures or information on a camera or computer so that they can be used in the future
secret	/ˈsiːkrət/	(adj)	not known or seen by other people
security	/sɪˈkjʊərəti/	(n)	the things that are done to keep someone or something safe
smartphone	/ˈsmɑːtfəʊn/	(n)	a mobile phone that can be used as a small computer and that connects to the internet
software	/ˈsɒftweə/	(n)	a program you use to control what a computer does
video game	/ˈvɪdiəʊ ˌɡeɪm/	(n)	a game in which the player controls moving pictures on a screen by pressing buttons
website	/ˈwebsaɪt/	(n)	a set of pages of information on the internet about a particular subject

Vocabulary	Pronunciation	Part of speech	Definition
UNIT 4			
almost	/ˈɔːlməʊst/	(adv)	not everything, but very close to it
careful	/ˈkeəfəl/	(adj)	paying attention to what you do so that you do not have an accident, make a mistake or damage something
cover	/ˈkʌvə/	(v)	to lie, or place, on the surface of something
dangerous	/ˈdeɪndʒərəs/	(adj)	can harm or hurt someone or something
decide	/dɪˈsaɪd/	(v)	to choose between one possibility or another
decrease	/ˈdiːkriːs/	(n)	a drop in the amount or size of something
decrease	/dɪˈkriːs/	(v)	to become less, or to make something become less
drop	/drɒp/	(v)	to decrease; to fall or go down
fall	/fɔːl/	(v)	to become less in number or amount
huge	/hjuːdʒ/	(adj)	extremely large in size or amount
increase	/ˈɪnkriːs/	(n)	a rise in amount or size of something
increase	/ɪnˈkriːs/	(v)	to get bigger or to make something bigger in size or amount
last	/lɑːst/	(v)	to continue for a period of time
lightning	/ˈlaɪtnɪŋ/	(n)	a flash of bright light in the sky during a storm

Vocabulary	Pronunciation	Part of speech	Definition
maximum ⊙	/ˈmæksɪməm/	(adj)	The maximum amount of something is the largest amount that is allowed or possible.
minimum ⊙	/ˈmɪnɪməm/	(adj)	The minimum amount of something is the smallest amount that is allowed or possible.
precipitation ⊙	/prɪsɪpɪˈteɪʃən/	(n)	rain or snow that falls to the ground
reach ⊙	/riːtʃ/	(v)	to arrive somewhere or to get to a particular point
rise ⊙	/raɪz/	(v)	to increase; to go up
shock ⊙	/ʃɒk/	(n)	a big, unpleasant surprise
thunder	/ˈθʌndə/	(n)	the sudden loud noise that comes after a flash of lightning
UNIT 5			
accident ⊙	/ˈæksɪdənt/	(n)	something bad that happens by mistake and that causes injury or damage
ancient ⊙	/ˈeɪnʃənt/	(adj)	from a long time ago; very old
challenging ⊙	/ˈtʃæləndʒɪŋ/	(adj)	difficult in a way that tests your ability
climb	/klaɪm/	(v)	go up something or onto the top of something
compete ⊙	/kəmˈpiːt/	(v)	to take part in a race or competition; to try to be more successful than someone else
competition ⊙	/ˌkɒmpəˈtɪʃən/	(n)	an organized event in which people try to win a prize by being the best

Vocabulary	Pronunciation	Part of speech	Definition
course	/kɔːs/	(n)	an area used for sporting events, such as racing or playing golf
fit	/fɪt/	(adj)	in good health; strong
participant	/pɑːˈtɪsɪpənt/	(n)	a person who takes part in an activity
strange	/streɪndʒ/	(adj)	not familiar; difficult to understand; different
swimming	/swɪmɪŋ/	(n)	sport where people move through water by moving their body
take place	/teɪk pleɪs/	(phr v)	to happen
throw	/θrəʊ/	(v)	to send something through the air, pushing it out of your hand

UNIT 6

Vocabulary	Pronunciation	Part of speech	Definition
advertise	/ˈædvətaɪz/	(v)	to tell people about a product or service, for example, in newspapers or on television, in order to persuade them to buy it
advice	/ədˈvaɪs/	(n)	an opinion that someone offers you about what you should do
apply	/əˈplaɪ/	(v)	ask officially for something, often by writing
colleague	/ˈkɒliːg/	(n)	someone that you work with
customer	/ˈkʌstəmə/	(n)	a person who buys things from a shop or business
department	/dɪˈpɑːtmənt/	(n)	part of a business or company
employ	/ɪmˈplɔɪ/	(v)	to pay someone to work or do a job for you

Vocabulary	Pronunciation	Part of speech	Definition
employee	/ɪm'plɔɪiː/	(n)	a worker
goal	/gəʊl/	(n)	something you want to do successfully in the future
hobby	/'hɒbi/	(n)	an activity you do for fun
introduce	/ˌɪntrə'djuːs/	(v)	to make something available to buy or use for the first time
manager	/'mænɪdʒə/	(n)	the person who organizes or leads a business
neat	/niːt/	(adj)	arranged well, with everything in its place
occupation	/ˌɒkjə'peɪʃən/	(n)	a job or career
office	/'ɒfɪs/	(n)	a place in a building where people work
organize	/'ɔːgənaɪz/	(v)	plan or arrange carefully
partner	/'pɑːtnə/	(n)	someone who runs or owns a business with another person
product	/'prɒdʌkt/	(n)	something a business makes and sells
result	/rɪ'zʌlt/	(n)	information that you find out from something, such as an exam, a scientific experiment or a medical test
run	/rʌn/	(v)	to manage or operate something
section	/'sekʃən/	(n)	one of the parts that something is divided into
set up	/set ʌp/	(phr v)	to create or establish (something) for a particular purpose

Vocabulary	Pronunciation	Part of speech	Definition
UNIT 7			
achieve	/ə'tʃiːv/	(v)	to succeed in doing something difficult
blind	/blaɪnd/	(adj)	not able to see
brave	/breɪv/	(adj)	not showing fear of dangerous or difficult situations
calm	/kɑːm/	(adj)	relaxed and not worried, frightened or excited
clever	/'klevə/	(adj)	able to learn and understand things quickly and easily
confident	/'kɒnfɪdənt/	(adj)	certain about your ability to do things well
difficult	/'dɪfɪkəlt/	(adj)	not friendly or easy to deal with
dream	/driːm/	(n)	something that you really want to do, be or have in the future
former	/'fɔːmə/	(adj)	before the present time or in the past
friendly	/'frendli/	(adj)	behaving in a pleasant, kind way towards someone
honest	/'ɒnɪst/	(adj)	truthful or able to be trusted; not likely to lie, cheat or steal
incredible	/ɪn'kredɪbl/	(adj)	impossible or very difficult to believe; amazing
inspire	/ɪn'spaɪə/	(v)	to make other people feel that they want to do something
intelligent	/ɪn'telɪdʒənt/	(adj)	able to learn and understand things easily; clever
kind	/kaɪnd/	(adj)	Kind people do things to help others and show that they care about them.

Vocabulary	Pronunciation	Part of speech	Definition
lazy	/'leɪzi/	(adj)	Someone who is lazy does not like working or using any effort.
look after	/lʊk 'ɑːftə/	(phr v)	to take care of someone or something by keeping them healthy or in a good condition
operation	/ˌɒpər'eɪʃən/	(n)	the process when doctors cut your body to repair it or to take something out
patient	/'peɪʃənt/	(adj)	able to stay calm and not get angry, especially when something takes a long time
reliable	/rɪ'laɪəbl/	(adj)	able to be trusted or believed
respect	/rɪ'spekt/	(v)	to like or to have a very good opinion of someone because of their knowledge, achievements, etc.
selfish	/'selfɪʃ/	(adj)	caring only about yourself and not other people
sensible	/'sensɪbl/	(adj)	showing good judgment
shy	/ʃaɪ/	(adj)	not confident, especially about meeting or talking to new people
stupid	/'stjuːpɪd/	(adj)	silly or not intelligent
talent	/'tælənt/	(n)	a natural ability to do something well
talented	/'tæləntɪd/	(adj)	showing natural ability in a particular area
train	/treɪn/	(v)	to prepare for a job, activity or sport by learning skills or by exercise

Vocabulary	Pronunciation	Part of speech	Definition
UNIT 8			
advance	/əd'vɑːns/	(n)	progress in the development or improvement of something
believe	/bɪ'liːv/	(v)	to think that something is true, or that what someone says is true
beyond	/bi'jɒnd/	(prep)	on the farther side of; at a farther distance than
conditions	/kən'dɪʃənz/	(n)	the situation in which people live, work or do things
crash	/kræʃ/	(v)	to hit something by accident, especially in a vehicle
entrepreneur	/ˌɒntrəprə'nɜː/	(n)	someone who starts their own business
evidence	/'evɪdəns/	(n)	something that makes you believe something is true
exist	/ɪg'zɪst/	(v)	be real, alive or present
explore	/ɪk'splɔː/	(v)	to travel to a new place to learn about it
particular	/pə'tɪkjələ/	(adj)	used to talk about one thing or person and not others
private	/'praɪvət/	(adj)	related to money or services controlled or supplied by a person or a company and not by the government
prove	/pruːv/	(v)	show that something is true
public	/'pʌblɪk/	(adj)	related to money or services controlled or supplied by the government and not by a person or a company

Vocabulary	Pronunciation	Part of speech	Definition
report	/rɪ'pɔːt/	(n)	a detailed examination of an event or situation
research	/rɪ'sɜːtʃ/	(n)	the detailed study of a subject to discover new information
study	/'stʌdi/	(n)	a report or piece of research that examines something in detail
suggest	/sə'dʒest/	(v)	to express an idea or plan for someone to consider
support	/sə'pɔːt/	(v)	help show that something is true
unlikely	/ʌn'laɪkli/	(adj)	not expected to happen; not probable
wonder	/'wʌndə/	(v)	think about something and try to understand it

VIDEO SCRIPTS

UNIT 1

Destination Jakarta

Narrator: Welcome to Jakarta, the capital of Indonesia and Southeast Asia's largest megacity. Jakarta is becoming more popular as a destination for tourists and business people every year.

Jakarta is home to over 9 million people. That number grows to 11 million by day, as 2 million people travel from nearby towns and villages to work here.

With its tall buildings and busy motorways, it's hard to believe that the great city of Jakarta grew from one small harbour and a few villages.

However, a visit to the old town of Batavia reveals the secrets of Jakarta's history.

Batavia was the centre of old Jakarta.

Its European-style buildings were built by the Dutch, who came here to buy and sell goods in the sixteenth century.

Sunda Kelapa harbour is where ships from Europe, China and India were filled with tea, coffee, spices, silk and so on to sell to the world. Here you can see Indonesian wooden sailing ships – still used today.

This is the Harbour Master's Tower – here the Dutch watched their ships entering and leaving the harbour.

If you're looking for a more modern attraction, Monas is the national monument. It stands 132 metres tall and at the top there is a golden flame. Below the tower you'll find the National Museum, where you can learn about 1.5 million years of Indonesian history.

Jakarta is also famous for its street food. You can find delicious fresh food such as *soto*, a soup of meat and vegetables, and *nasi goreng*, a fried rice dish.

If you plan a trip in December, don't miss the fireworks display at Lagoon Beach – the perfect way to celebrate the New Year at a new destination.

UNIT 2

New Year celebrations across the UK

Crowds: Four ... three ... two ... one ... (*cheers*)

Commentator: Yet again, London said goodbye to the year in spectacular fashion. 12,000 fireworks lit up the perfectly clear London sky.

More than 100,000 people lined the River Thames. Many had waited hours for their front-row view.

Interviewee 1: Very, very great ... amazing! Awesome!

Interviewee 2: I come from Buenos Aires, Argentina, erm ... it was really worth it. I don't regret it at all.

Interviewee 3: We queued, we waited here for three hours but it was really worth it, I liked it, we all liked it.

Journalist: New Year's Eve, with the London Eye as the backdrop, still continues to draw media coverage from around the world and, of course, the huge crowds. But it's not just the capital, as cities around the UK bring in the New Year in style.

Commentator: It's party time again, and this is how it shapes up – in a line. 8,000 people snaked along Edinburgh's Princes Street in a torch-lit procession as the city's three-day Hogmanay festival kicked off.

Edinburgh's spectacular peaks at New Year's midnight hour when five minutes of fireworks are laid on for a crowd of 75,000 people. This was the warm-up of the night before.

Interviewee: Edinburgh's Hogmanay is always special. It's a unique Scottish celebration. It's the only three-day New Year's celebration festival, erm ... of New Year in the world.

Commentator: They are the pyrotechnics that punctuate the end of the old year and start of the new. A time for looking backwards, looking forwards and for looking up.

UNIT 3

Predictive advertising

Narrator: Every time we make a phone call, search online or buy something, we leave information, or data, about our habits. And the amount of data is getting bigger, by 2.5 billion gigabytes every day. All that data is worth a lot of money.

Mike Baker is a 'data hunter'. He collects data. He thinks this information is changing the way we live and the way we do business.

A few years ago, Mike decided to help advertisers. Why should companies wait for people to find their ads when it was now possible to bring personalized ads to everyone?

Then he had another idea. If companies had enough information about people's past activities, could they use this information to predict their future activities?

Mike felt that they could – that they could predict what people might want to buy. But it was difficult because there was too much data. He needed a program to understand and use the data.

And he wanted to be able to use the data fast – to be able to predict what people wanted to buy, before they even knew it. But he needed help.

So Mike found a partner with a superfast program. Together, they made the program do what Mike wanted it to do. The program looks at data very quickly and finds clues about what people might want to buy.

Then it sends them personalized ads. For example, it might learn that you like Italian food and are interested in cars, so it sends you ads about those things.

We now live in a world of personalized ads. Yes, you can choose not to have personalized ads, but you can't get away from ads completely. So maybe it's better to see ads for things you like than for things you don't care about.

UNIT 4

Tornadoes

Narrator: In the middle of the United States, spring brings warm, wet air from the south, making things perfect for one of the most extreme weather events on Earth – tornadoes. That's why this part of the country is called Tornado Alley.

Some years are worse than others, and 2011 was one of the worst ever.

Man: Did you see that? The whole house came apart!

Narrator: That year, in the town of Joplin, Missouri, a dangerous tornado killed more than 160 people.

But although we know a lot about the science of tornadoes, we still can't predict exactly when or where they will happen.

Josh Wurman is a weather scientist. He and his team are studying how thunderstorms produce tornadoes.

Seventy-five percent of thunderstorms don't produce tornadoes, but twenty-five percent of them do. But which thunderstorms will do it?

To answer this question, Josh and his team need to get information from as many tornadoes as they can during the spring. To find the storms, Josh uses a Doppler radar scanner. It can show him what's going on inside a thunderstorm, which gives him important information about what starts a tornado.

Josh now knows where to look, but finding the right storm is always difficult. Then, after 1,000 miles of driving, they find the right one. But the team has to move fast because tornadoes come and go very quickly.

And there's the tornado they're looking for.

Woman: There we go. That's what it's about.

Man 1: Yeah.

Man 2: There she is.

Man 1: It's a beauty.

Man 2: It's a beauty.

Man on radio: Be careful. Be careful.

Narrator: This huge tornado is less than a mile away from the team.

Its winds are spinning up to 200 miles per hour.

But less than 30 minutes after the tornado appeared, it dies. It was one of more than 1,200 tornadoes in this part of Tornado Alley since the beginning of spring.

UNIT 5

▶ A 96-year-old bungee jumper

Narrator: This is the Bloukrans Bridge in South Africa. At 216 metres high, it is one of the highest bungee jumps in the world. Mohr Keet made history here by becoming the world's oldest bungee jumper at the age of 96.

Bungee jumping looks dangerous, and it can be. Although ropes don't often break, jumpers are sometimes injured. After the jumper falls, the bungee rope suddenly pulls their body back and up. This can damage the eyes, the back or the neck and can even kill you. For a man of Mohr's age, the chances of being injured must certainly increase.

But this wasn't Mohr's first bungee jump – in fact, he had done it twice before. His first jump was when he was 88. Then he did it again at 93.

Guide: It's strong enough, I promise you. It's strong enough.

Narrator: So didn't Mohr get scared?

MK: Yes, of course I'm scared.

Interviewer: But, you don't mind? About the fear?

MK: No, I like it.

Instructors: Five, four, three, two, one – bungee!

Narrator: Mohr did not know he was going to break a world record when he jumped. He said he did it for the challenge and the experience.

MK: Very frightening, very exciting, very thrilling. When you jump, of course, it's the roar of the wind in your ears, it's deafening. The wind was blowing very hard, gusting, and you jerk, and the rope, the cable would shake like that, and it really shook you up! Hanging there and it shaking you and then shaking you ... that was a definite experience.

Narrator: After his jump, doctors checked the 96-year-old and found him in perfect health.

Interviewer: What about when you're on the edge and you're so scared? What do you think about?

MK: No, you don't think. You just ... You just do it.

UNIT 6

Amazon's fulfilment centre

Narrator: Today Amazon is the world's largest online store. But its first warehouse was a small basement in Seattle, Washington.

Now, with more than 100 million items for sale on its website, Amazon has many large warehouses around the world called 'fulfilment centres'. How do they find your item? Only the central computer knows where everything is. Any item can be on any shelf.

In fact, their location is random so that workers don't take the wrong item.

After you order and pay for an item online, an Amazon worker walks through the warehouse and finds your kitchen item or your cute toy.

The computer then tells the workers the right size of the box.

Finally, your name and address goes on the box before it leaves the fulfilment centre.

UNIT 7

The gold prospector

Narrator: Vince Thurkettle is looking for gold in the Little Ouse River, in the east of England. Finding gold is not just a hobby for Vince, it's his job.

After 12 hours' hard work, he's found a piece! And it's almost pure gold.

Vince became a gold prospector after he met another prospector one day. The man told him all about where and how to find gold. Vince decided to leave his safe but boring office job and start looking for gold. His new job has taken him to every part of the world, including Alaska, Australia and Finland.

All he needed to get started was a shovel and a gold pan, which is just a metal or plastic dish. He uses this pan to carefully wash the stones from the bottom of the river. Gold is very heavy, so it always goes to the bottom of the river. And because gold is so heavy, it doesn't move very far down river – so where Vince finds one piece of gold, there is usually more nearby.

It's not an easy life, though; the work is hard and tiring. Vince works 12 hours a day whether it is hot or cold, raining or even snowing.

Most of the pieces of gold Vince finds are very small. On a good day, he can find about £200 worth of gold. But he is not usually that lucky. Some days he finds just a few pounds' worth, or even nothing at all.

When Vince worked in an office he earned around £50,000 a year; now he only earns about £12,000 – only enough for the things he needs. But Vince doesn't do it for the money – being a gold prospector is his dream job. He says he wishes more people would follow their dreams.

UNIT 8

Going to the International Space Station

Narrator: Most people drive or take a bus, train or subway to work.

But Sunita Williams is different.

Every morning she gets up, takes her dog for a walk and gets ready for work. But sometimes when she goes to work, her vehicle is very unusual. Yes, it takes her 15–20 minutes with traffic to drive her car two miles to the office in Houston, Texas.

But we're not talking about that vehicle or that office.

She has a special vehicle she takes to a different office, and traffic's not a problem.

Captain Sunita Williams is an American astronaut. In 2012 she spent four months in a very special office – the International Space Station.

She travelled to the space station in this Russian Soyuz rocket.

The trip was 250 miles, straight up.

The trip to space took just nine minutes.

That's half the time it usually takes Sunita to drive to work.

Sunita Williams travelled in a tiny capsule on top of hundreds of tons of rocket power.

After she, Russian cosmonaut Yuri Malenchenko and Japanese astronaut Akihiko Hoshide climbed the stairs and rode the elevator to the top, they went inside. Then it was time to blast off for the International Space Station.

Man: T-minus ten, nine, eight, seven, six, five, four, three, two, one, lift-off. Lift-off of the Soyuz TMA05M, carrying Suni Williams, Yuri Malenchenko and Aki Hoshide on a journey to the International Space Station.

ACKNOWLEDGEMENTS

The authors and publishers acknowledge the following sources of copyright material and are grateful for the permissions granted. While every effort has been made, it has not always been possible to identify the sources of all the material used, or to trace all copyright holders. If any omissions are brought to our notice, we will be happy to include the appropriate acknowledgements on reprinting and in the next update to the digital edition, as applicable.

Key: B = Below, C = Centre, L = Left, R = Right, T = Top.

Text
Graphs on p. 93 adapted from 'Amman, Amman Governorate Monthly Climate Average, Jordan'. Copyright © worldweatheronline. Reproduced with kind permission.

Photos
All images are sourced from Getty Images.

pp. 14–15: Danita Delimont/Gallo Images; p. 23 (T): Andrew Bret Wallis/The Image Bank; p. 23 (B): Zubin Shroff/The Image Bank; p. 32: Jose Fuste Raga/Corbis Documentary; pp. 36–37: Saha Entertainment/The Image Bank; p. 37 (L): Per-Andre Hoffmann/LOOK-foto; p. 37 (C): Rich-Joseph Facun/arabianEye; p. 37 (R): laflor/E+; p. 41 (pinata): Sollina Images/The Image Bank; p. 41 (noodles): Chia Hsien Lee/EyeEm; p. 41 (gift): emmaduckworth/RooM; p. 41 (new year): Dan Kitwood/Getty Images News; p. 41 (age day): Andia/Universal Images Group; p. 43: Aleksandr_Vorobev/iStock Editorial/Getty Images Plus; p. 44 (T): MARWAN NAAMANI/AFP; p. 44 (B): John Elk/Lonely Planet Images; p. 49: vinhdav/iStock Editorial/Getty Images Plus; p. 53: Peter Zelei Images/Moment; pp. 58–59: wiratgasem/Moment; p. 63 (L): Hero Images; p. 63 (R): andresr/E+; p. 75: Yuri_Arcurs/E+; pp. 80–81: Pavliha/E+; p. 81 (a): Bryan Mullennix/The Image Bank; p. 81 (b): Ariadne Van Zandbergen/Lonely Planet Images; p. 81 (c): BOISVIEUX Christophe/hemis.fr; p. 81 (d): Andre Gallant/Photographer's Choice; p. 89: Frank Krahmer/DigitalVision; pp. 102–103: Roland Hemmi/Design Pics; p. 107: Morgan Hancock/Action Plus; p. 108 (L): PETER PARKS/AFP; p. 108 (R): VisitBritain/Andrew Pickett; p. 112: Mike Hewitt/Getty Images Sport; p. 125 (T): Chesnot/Getty Images News; p. 125 (B):Amanda Edwards/WireImage; p. 133: James Leynse/Corbis Historical; pp. 146–147: Tom Bonaventure/Photographer's Choice RF; p. 147 (L): Sean Gallup/Getty Images News; p. 147 (C): Tim Graham/Tim Graham Photo Library; p. 147 (R): ullstein bild Dtl.; p. 151: Sacramento Bee/Tribune News Service; p. 155 (T): Sean Gallup/Getty Images News; p. 155 (B): Sean Drakes/CON/LatinContent Editorial; p. 164: AFP; pp. 168–169: NASA/Handout/Getty Images News; p. 173 (T): ROBYN BECK/AFP; p. 173 (B): Bloomberg; p. 176: Stocktrek Images; p. 179: Inigo Cia/Moment.

The following image is from other image library:
pp. 124–125: Pavel L Photo and Video/Shutterstock.

Front cover photography by Copyright Xinzheng. All Rights Reserved/Moment.

Video stills
All below stills are sourced from Getty Images.

p. 16 (a): Bob Chappell and John Alfirevich/Image Bank Film; p. 16 (b, d): Bloomberg Video – Footage/Bloomberg; p. 16 (c): srisadonous/Creatas Video+/Getty Images Plus; p. 38: Sky News/Film Image Partner; p. 104 (a): Gsmotion/Photolibrary Video; p. 104 (b, c, d), p. 148: Barcroft Media Video.

The following stills are sourced from other libraries.

p. 60, p. 82, p. 126, p. 170: BBC Worldwide Learning.

Illustrations
p. 112, p. 119: Ben Hasler; p. 114, p. 115: Fiona Gowen.

Videos
Videos supplied by BBC Worldwide Learning and Getty Images.

ITN; Bob Chappell and John Alfirevich/Image Bank Film; Bloomberg Video – Footage/Bloomberg; Fadil Aziz/DigitalVision; srisadonous/Creatas Video+/Getty Images Plus; AFP Footage; Sky News/Film Image Partner; Barcroft Media – Footage/Barcroft Media Video; Gsmotion/Photolibrary Video; Roberto Machado Noa/LightRocket; Feature Story News – Footage/Getty Images Editorial Footage; Faithfulshot – Footage/Getty Images Editorial Footage; Tribune Broadcasting – Anna Burkart; CrowdSpark; TRAVELXP HD/Image Bank Film; Fraser Hall/Image Bank Film; Manakin/iStock/Getty Images Plus; Smithsonian; BBC Worldwide learning.

Corpus
Development of this publication has made use of the Cambridge English Corpus (CEC). The CEC is a multi-billion word computer database of contemporary spoken and written English. It includes British English, American English and other varieties of English. It also includes the Cambridge Learner Corpus, developed in collaboration with the University of Cambridge ESOL Examinations. Cambridge University Press has built up the CEC to provide evidence about language use that helps to produce better language teaching materials.

Cambridge Dictionaries
Cambridge dictionaries are the world's most widely used dictionaries for learners of English. The dictionaries are available in print and online at dictionary.cambridge.org. Copyright © Cambridge University Press, reproduced with permission.

Typeset by emc design ltd.

UNLOCK SECOND EDITION ADVISORY PANEL

We would like to thank the following ELT professionals all around the world for their support, expertise and input throughout the development of *Unlock* Second Edition:

Adnan Abu Ayyash, Birzeit University, Palestine	Takayuki Hara, Kagoshima University, Japan	Megan Putney, Dhofar University, Oman
Bradley Adrain, University of Queensland, Australia	Esengül Hasdemir, Atilim University, Turkey	Wayne Rimmer, United Kingdom
Sarah Ali, Nottingham Trent International College (NTIC), United Kingdom	Irina Idilova, Moscow Institute of Physics and Technology, Russia	Sana Salam, TED University, Turkey
Ana Maria Astiazaran, Colegio Regis La Salle, Mexico	Meena Inguva, Sultan Qaboos University, Oman	Setenay Şekercioglu, Işık University, Turkey
Asmaa Awad, University of Sharjah, United Arab Emirates	Vasilios Konstantinidis, Prince Sultan University, Kingdom of Saudi Arabia	Robert B. Staehlin, Morioka University, Japan
Jesse Balanyk, Zayed University, United Arab Emirates	Andrew Leichsenring, Tamagawa University, Japan	Yizhi Tang, Xueersi English, TAL Group, China
Lenise Butler, Universidad del Valle de México, Mexico	Alexsandra Minic, Modern College of Business and Science, Oman	Valeria Thomson, Muscat College, Oman
Esin Çağlayan, Izmir University of Economics, Turkey	Daniel Newbury, Fuji University, Japan	Amira Traish, University of Sharjah, United Arab Emirates
Matthew Carey, Qatar University, Qatar	Güliz Özgürel, Yaşar University, Turkey	Poh Leng Wendelkin, INTO City, University of London, United Kingdom
Eileen Dickens, Universidad de las Américas, Mexico	Özlem Perks, Istanbul Ticaret University, Turkey	Yoee Yang, The Affiliated High School of SCNU, China
Mireille Bassam Farah, United Arab Emirates	Claudia Piccoli, Harmon Hall, Mexico	Rola Youhia, University of Adelaide College, Australia
Adriana Ghoul, Arab American University, Palestine	Tom Pritchard, University of Edinburgh, United Kingdom	Long Zhao, Xueersi English, TAL Group, China
Burçin Gönülsen, Işık University, Turkey		